To Chi -
always
with courage
Cheers
XO !

HAVE
BREAST CANCER,
WILL TRAVEL

Postcards From My Journey

Thanks for
all the MOPS love.

by JAN ALLEN

These postcards are dedicated to my loving family and friends who stood by me in the
"Year of the Pink Warrior,"

to my incredible team of oncologists, surgeons, radiation and chemotherapy techs and the countless compassionate nurses at Scripps Green Cancer Center,

to our amazing Hyatt family,

to the awesome Allen brothers who were "bald ready" to stand alongside me,

to my biggest blessings, Zack and Savannah, who are forever my light in life,

to my "miracle" Scott who is forever my rock,

to all my remarkable fellow warriors—some of whom have fought and won the cancer battle,

and those who have lost their lives to the disease, with fervent hope that fewer of our future generations will have a battle to fight.

Deltiology
(Collection of Postcards)

Foreword xi
The Journey Begins xiii

1.   Greetings! From A Pink Warrior..................... 17
2.   Can You Say, "Wake Me Up At Thanksgiving?"........ 19
3.   Have Patience, Have Patience, Don't Be
     In Such A Hurry.. 20
4.   It's The Little Things................................. 22
5.   Have Breast Cancer, Will Travel 24
6.   Strength In Numbers, Part 1.......................... 26
7.   Strength In Numbers, Part 2.......................... 28
8.   Plan For The Worst, Hope For The Best 31
9.   It's Out! Let The Nursing Begin. 33
10. Never Been Hit By A Truck Before 34
11. "Modesty, Shmodesty" 36
12. My Heart Is Full....................................... 39
13. Returning To The Scene Of The Crime............... 41
14. Celebration Of A Sweet Life 43
15. Do I Really Want To Know? And Why Didn't
     Anyone Tell Me That Earlier?........................ 45
16. New Weapon Unveiled In Battle Of Pink
     Warrior VS. The Carcinoma!.......................... 47
17. Does A Chocolate Shake Qualify As A
     "Clear Liquid?" Of Course! 49
18. "Let's Talk Chemo!"................................... 50
19. March Madness 52
20. "Nothing Is Quite As Funny As The Unintended
     Humor Of Reality".................................... 53

21. Storm Or Sunshine? What Do I Need? 55
22. "Good" Friday? 57
23. "Former Flight Attendant Returns To The Airport
     Again, And Again, And Again, And Yet Again!" 60
24. Heaven At The Hyatt 62
25. Who Is That Cat In The HAT? 65
26. Storms In The Forecast 69
27. Happy Hour On Friday! 72
28. I Am A Lover, Not A Fighter! 75
29. "There Ain't Much Fun In Medicine, But
     There's A Heck Of A Lot Of Medicine In Fun" 77
30. Just A Verse For Today 81
31. The Hangover 82
32. It's Working... 83
33. What I Am Thankful For Today 84
34. I'm "Rash-a-licious!" 85
35. Thoughts Of Mom 86
36. The Pink Plagues 90
37. Top Ten List 92
38. Never Underestimate The Healing Power Of
     Ice Cream 94
39. There's A Time For Everything 96
40. Full Circle 98
41. What A Wonderful Week! 99
42. 2 Down, 2 To Go! 102
43. Me — A Zebra? NOT A Turkey! 103
44. Rockin' That Wig 105
45. Hair Today, Gone Tomorrow 107
46. It's Memorial Day! 109
47. Itchy and Scratchy 111
48. Happy Hour Monday! 112
49. Not A Texas Longhorn Fan, But 113
50. A Boo-Yah For Bette 115
51. Twitchy, Itchy, Witchy Chickie 117
52. The Soothing Sun 119
53. 'Twas The Night Before My Last Chemo 121
54. Disturbing The Peace 124

55. Turning A Corner....................................126
56. Stop And Smell The Daisies 127
57. From Wigs And Weight Gain To Hormones
     And Hot Flashes...................................129
58. Tickled Pink......................................131
59. "Scripps Ink" Tatts Up Pink Warrior!..............134
60. An Old Scar.......................................136
61. 4th Down, 32 To Go 139
62. Attitude Is Everything! 141
63. It's Five O'Clock Somewhere... 142
64. Mystery Of The Missing Lashes 143
65. It's A Marathon...................................145
66. Chicken Fried.....................................147
67. Sheepie — The Sequel: "Unlikely Hero
     Counteracts Attack Of The Linear Accelerator!".....150
68. With Bells On.....................................152
69. Taking The Highway To... 154
70. One Of The 200,000 156
71. Vulnerable..158
72. I Left My Heart ... And A Few Other Things
     In Panama City Beach! 160
73. "Dude, Where's My Legs?"..........................162
74. AMA-zing!!!.......................................165
75. Just Do It!.......................................168
76. DaVinci Is My Friend 170
77. Hormones Gone Haywire 171
78. Surprised By Joy..................................174
79. The Year Of The What?.............................177
80. I Need New Shoes! 179
81. First Hair Cut....................................182
82. Tsunami Survival..................................184

The Journey Continues................................191
Appendices 193

Foreword

$\mathcal{W}$ay back in a time that I am certainly too young to remember, a freshly-crowned Valedictorian hopped on her first ever plane ride from her tiny farm town of New Haven, Indiana all the way to visit her sister who was living as a missionary in Nigeria. Before cell phones, before email, her older brothers simply had to trust that their baby sister would have someone at the airport in Africa to escort her to the tiny village where she would find her sister. Luckily, Jan Allen did manage to find her sister in a foreign land and take the first of what would be many journeys to come.

Just as luckily, she made it through that journey—although one particularly nasty boar tried its best to stop that—and eventually had some kids. Of which I happen to be one. It's nearly impossible for me to imagine my mom as that nervous kid going to Nigeria. For as long as I can remember, my mom has been one of the strongest and most confident people I've ever met. Throughout my childhood, she went through more than her fair share of journeys. From raising me and my sister by working every odd job she could find, diving headfirst into love again, moving to an island small enough to drive across in less than hour and—as you probably guessed from the title of this book—being diagnosed with and beating breast cancer. Through it all, my mom remained my mom: loving, happy and impossibly bright.

I don't know a single person that could go through everything that my mom did and come out the other side as an even more electrifyingly cheerful and caring person the way she did. Watching her for the past 22 years has been incredible. Seeing a person roll with every punch and continue to grow and care for those around them is a truly awe-inspiring sight. I'm lucky enough to have been able to tag along for the ride and her courage is what drove me to venture off on my own journey and I'll never be able to thank her enough for it.

I can only hope that the story of courage that follows this meager introduction inspires you to follow your journey with as much courage as she did.

– Zachary Keegan Baker

The Journey Begins.

2010 started off like any other year. The usual resolutions made, the month-by-month planning of work events and activities and the anticipation of family and friends' visits to our home in San Diego. But quickly all these plans were dashed and a new impromptu "trip" was in the works. A trip that would take every ounce of energy and determination I had: a journey through a breast cancer diagnosis.

As recommended by my family doctor, I had a mammogram when I turned 40. Like so many women, all was in order; and with no family history of breast cancer, I neglected my annual screening for 4 years. When I showed up in Dr. S's La Jolla office in November 2009 as a new patient, she wouldn't take "no" for an answer and insisted I get screened right away, so I had my second mammogram. I never imagined that the timing of that screening probably saved my life.

Just before the Christmas holidays, I received a call from the office saying "something didn't look quite right" on the right breast and that the office would like to compare my new mammogram with the slides from my old mammogram 4 years ago. Well, never one to panic, I just assumed what they were "seeing" on my mammogram was a cyst or calcium deposit. Several of my friends and family had these and I figured I did, too. I would try to get the old mammogram slide for the doctor but *after* the holidays! No rush. Meanwhile, I tried and tried to feel a lump on the right side, but I couldn't feel anything. And so I concluded, it must be nothing.

After the family left in early January, I figured I should track down the old mammogram and have it sent to my doctor's office. I knew that she would keep "pestering" me until I got it. Soon after her office received it, the nurse called again. I needed to schedule a pinpoint mammogram and an ultrasound. The spot they saw on my right breast hadn't been there 4 years ago and they wanted to check it out. Okay, I thought, no problem. I was still certain it was a cyst—nothing to worry about.

A week or so later, I did the pinpoint mammogram and the ultrasound on the same day. By the time I got into the office for these procedures in early February I thought I could feel a small lump on the underside of my right breast. When I got to the appointment, I asked the nurse right away if that was the location that the doctor was concerned about and was shocked to find out that it was. I was certain that the lump must have been growing because there had been nothing there in December, but I remained convinced it was nothing. As I lay on the table that day while the tech did the ultrasound, I had my first thought that things weren't as they should be. She asked for another tech to come into the exam room and kept going over and over that same spot. The doctor finally came in and said that my lymph nodes looked good but the lump was "concerning." I would need a biopsy.

Friday, February 19, 2010 I had the biopsy. A long, skinny, sharp device similar to a needle is inserted through the skin into the tissue of the "lump" and when it is pulled out a portion of the tissue comes out too. This tissue is then turned over to the lab to see if it is cancerous or benign. The doctor had a particularly rough time retrieving the tissue. I would later find out that this can be a sign that the tumor is cancerous, but I didn't know that when I was having the procedure. I had to wait all weekend long to get the results.

The phone rang at 9:05am on Monday, February 22. Because my husband was worried about me, he had stopped back home from work just then to see if I had news. He would be my "rock" — no matter what. On the phone was a nurse from my doctor's office, I held my breath. Matter of factly, she uttered the words, "Your biopsy showed evidence of malignancy. You have breast cancer. Your tumor is an invasive ductile carcinoma." I think she continued to speak to me for 5 minutes or more, communicating all the "next steps," such as making appointments with a medical oncologist, radiation oncologist and surgeon. Dumbfounded, I didn't really hear her further instructions.

I had just received the ticket for a trip I never wanted to take.

Postcard 1
Greetings! From A Pink Warrior

Sunday, February 28, 2010, 6:05 p.m.

"Pink Warrior?" My husband Scott has used a "Black Warrior" for years at work, a certain type of pencil made by Mirado. He loves to write and do his work with a pencil but he insists on this *particular type* of pencil. If it's not a Black Warrior, it's no good. Since we received the shocking breast cancer diagnosis, Scott decided that we need to be "Pink Warriors" now. I like it because I know that Scott has accomplished a lot with his Black Warrior. He has balanced our checkbook, completed hundreds of "to-do" lists, and successfully managed million dollar renovations and hotel operations—all with the assistance of his Black Warrior. Together we have concluded that it's time that God uses me (and Scott) to accomplish whatever He needs to do as His "Pink" Warriors. He has brought us to this day and will be with us through the journey wherever it may lead.

Gosh, it's nearly one week already since I found out I have breast cancer. I have a "high grade ductile carcinoma" about 1 1/2 cm in diameter on my right breast. How can that be?!? I was so certain that it would be a fluid filled cyst or even a benign tumor. No one in my immediate family has ever had cancer, so believe me, I was not expecting the diagnosis. My wonderfully supportive husband took me for a long walk at a beautiful beach here in San Diego the afternoon we found out. We talked it out and cried a little, but also realized how blessed we are to catch it early and that the tumor is small.

Later last week we met with the surgeon and talked over some options. It looks like a lumpectomy, some radiation and chemo will be the treatment plan. I don't really know much more than that right now. I see the radiation oncologist tomorrow and the surgery will be scheduled after that. One day at a time...

Scott cooked up a fabulous dinner tonight. A healthy and yummy dinner. I'd better go eat. This Pink Warrior will need lots of energy!

> *Put on your sword, O mighty warrior! You are so glorious, so majestic! In your majesty, ride out to victory, defending truth, humility, and justice. Go forth to perform awe-inspiring deeds!*Psalm 45:3-4 NLT

Postcard 2

Can You Say "Wake Me Up At Thanksgiving?"

Monday, March 1, 2010, 2:33 p.m.

Today was my highly anticipated first oncologist appointment. The details are overwhelming and I would have been much happier if I had never had to go.

I guess our plan is to fix everything and to fix it for good, which means I am gonna get the deluxe, extra-special, tried and true, golden ticket, double dose of everything! Whoopee! Because of the high grade of the tumor and because of my "young" (LOL) age, they want to cover all the bases to be sure it won't recur. I guess I do like that idea! BUT I don't like the idea of 4-5 months of chemo, 7 weeks of radiation, and some hormone therapy thrown in, just to round everything out.

My surgery date can't some soon enough for me. It's tentatively scheduled in 2 weeks, but they are looking for an opportunity to move it up. I pray that they find one.
Oh and yay! The nurse gave Scott the go-ahead to get me into fighting shape, so I think I have a date with a medicine ball sometime around 5 a.m.!

> *"I keep dreaming of a future, a future with a*
> *long and healthy life, not lived in the shadow of*
> *cancer but in the light."*   Patrick Swayze

Postcard 3
Have Patience, Have Patience, Don't Be In Such A Hurry...

Tuesday, March 2, 2010, 3:40 p.m.

I remember those words from a song in a Sunday School Musical number that I sang when I was a kid. It came to mind today as I was waiting anxiously for the surgical nurse to call and schedule my lumpectomy. I was reminded to take a deep breath and calm down. My surgery is tentatively scheduled for the 15th. Unfortunately, this is in 2 weeks and it is scheduled when Scott needs to be in Chicago. His company has executive meetings infrequently and it is important for him to be there. Of course, he will stay home if he needs to, but I really don't want him to have to change his plans. I am praying that an earlier slot opens up!

Today I am already feeling better than yesterday about the treatment plan. Yesterday "therapies until Thanksgiving" seemed unthinkable... today they seem like a blessing. The fact that doctors and researchers have developed such excellent ways to battle such a scary disease is certainly a reason to be grateful. I kept my date with the "medicine ball" this morning and it felt good. I have been listening to an upbeat playlist at the gym (the choice on the TV at 5:15 a.m. is pretty much news, news or more news and in case you haven't watched news in a while, it is pretty depressing). It's incredible how music lifts the soul.

It's a beautiful day here and I enjoyed Starbucks with a dear friend this morning... God is good.

Wait for the Lord; be strong and take heart and wait for the Lord.   Psalm 27:14

Postcard 4
It's The Little Things.

Wednesday, March 3, 2010, 3:00 p.m.

First off, prayers answered! I found out today that my surgery will be next Wednesday, March 10, in the morning. Now Scott can feel free go on his trip for work the following week, by which time I will be safely in the hands of my wonderful and capable sister and niece! Yay! Tomorrow at 11:30 I will be having some pre-op appointments in preparation for next week.

This postcard is titled "It's The Little Things" because I want to share something incredible that happened to me yesterday. It was a small but powerful thing. I know my Father in heaven was smiling. Those of you who have kids know the thrill of knowing your child wants a special toy and knowing that you've already secretly bought it for them and they just don't know it yet.

Well, yesterday I went into CVS to buy some necessary toiletries and as I passed the office supplies (a weakness of mine) I saw this really cute small notebook. It was brown with multicolored polka-dots... really cute! I knew I really didn't NEED it, but I kept thinking of reasons why I should buy it, i.e. "I need a smaller notebook to take notes at Dr.'s appointments," "it would match a larger notebook that I already have," "I have so much to get done before my treatments, that would be perfect to keep a to-do list." As all these thoughts were running through my head, another small voice was saying, "You and Scott have decided to stop discretionary spending until we see what the medical bills will be," "What about that big tax bill looming?," "You don't really need it, you WANT it!"

In the end my sensibilities won, and I cashed out without the adorable notebook. Just a couple hours later, Scott came home from the office with our mail. He had some really wonderful cards from family and friends (so much appreciated) and a small package from a dear friend from church. Imagine my joy, when I opened it and found some pretty pink "breast cancer awareness" pens and the EXACT notebook I had passed up at the store. I know my Father was smiling as He blessed me through a sweet friend with exactly what my little heart had longed for. How great is our God.

> *Take delight in the Lord, and he will give you the*
> *desires of your heart.*   Psalm 37:4

Postcard 5
Have Breast Cancer, Will Travel

Thursday, March 4, 2010, 4:12 p.m.

Now I'm sure you probably realize that I have already had a ton of appointments with doctors, labs, ultrasounds, on and on.... and this is playing havoc with my calendar and Scott's as well (since he has been by my side with a notebook at each visit!) I know that what we have experienced so far is nothing compared to what lies ahead in 2010. Today, however, imagine my surprise when I went to the surgical scheduling nurse and she handed me something I am very familiar with, something I have used since my days as a flight attendant 20 years ago and something I deal with on a regular basis in my career now: she handed me a folder and tucked neatly inside was my "Scripps Appointment ITINERARY." Ah, finally, something in this cancer world I can relate too, something I am comfortable with! I can handle an itinerary! As overwhelming as it was to see the 10 upcoming appointments already listed I felt some immediate relief, a brief glimmer of excitement even. Having an "Itinerary," means going on a wonderful trip! Of course I know in reality it is going to be a long and difficult journey for me and for Scott, but I took a little comfort today in the fact that all I have to do is follow my "itinerary" into the unknown, something this travel professional can do with confidence.

Our concern now is that my surgery on Wednesday would go smoothly and, most importantly, that when they do the pathology during the procedure that there will be ZERO cancer cells in my lymph nodes.

(The five-year relative survival for women with stage I breast cancer is 100 percent. [Source: American Cancer Society–last revised 6/10/2015.] This means that women with stage I breast cancer were, on average, just as likely as women in the general population to live five more years. Note: The percentages go down according to the increased stage of the cancer.)

Luggage Tag created from a photo of Jan in Berlin
circa 1990 as a Pan Am Flight Attendant

Postcard 6
Strength In Numbers, Part 1

Saturday, March 6, 2010, 5:13 p.m.

About a month ago, I made plans to host a little dinner party last night. Since receiving my diagnosis about 2 weeks ago, I gave a brief thought to canceling. But after a little contemplation, I decided to go ahead with the party. The idea behind the dinner party was to give some really wonderful moms, who have preschoolers at home, a night out. I truly have a heart for these women that day after day, cook breakfast, lunch and dinner for their families, wake up in the middle of the night with infants or tolerate toddlers in their own beds, drag 2 or 3 little ones to the grocery and Target, and then rush home for nap time. These ladies are heroes in their families but get very little reward or acknowledgment. Last night was to be a treat for them. It ended up being a treat for me, and exactly what the doctor ordered! I cannot tell you what a blessing it was just to sit around our dinner table, talking, laughing, and eating. The dinner was phenomenal. And, no, I am not raving about my own skill in the kitchen. Scott took over and prepared the most yummy stuffed pork loin and couscous with crab-stuffed mushrooms as an appetizer. All I had to do was boil the carrots! He sat in another room while the 8 of us enjoyed our time together and later he said he had never heard such a thing. He compared it to a bunch of mother hens, just clucking away: 4 different conversations at once, mixed with laughter and some tears. I cannot begin to tell you how uplifting the evening was for me; it gave me strength for the week ahead. Whatever you are facing this week, I hope you also will find strength in the support of caring family and friends.

> *I am going to keep on being glad, for I know that*
> *as you pray for me, and as the Holy Spirit helps*
> *me, this is all going to turn out for my good.*
> Philippians 1:19 The Living Bible Translation

Postcard 7
Strength In Numbers, Part 2

Sunday, March 7, 2010, 8:38 p.m.

"Chemotherapy"... CHEMO... "Systemic Treatment"... CHEMO.... "Your Personal Drug Recipe".. CHEMO... it doesn't matter what you call it, I think most of you are like me—when you say "chemo," you might as well say "bald," because it's the first thing that comes to mind. When I received my diagnosis, I researched online the possible treatments because I thought the tumor was small. I believed the most likely treatment would be "lumpectomy followed by radiation." Not exactly a party, but hey, at least I thought no CHEMO! To me, that equated to NO baldness. Whew!

But guess what? After the last few doctors appointments I am beginning to get the idea that the chemo thing is going to be a part of my future. And actually, I am almost convinced that it is a good idea—cleaning out my blood and ridding it of cancer cells sounds like a great idea! But the baldness doesn't.

I am not quite sure why I am so attached to my hair. So far I feel that I have come to terms with pretty much everything else I have to look forward to on this journey. I know it won't be easy and I feel very naive about what I am going to go through, but NOTHING causes that sick feeling in the pit of my stomach like losing my hair. Maybe it's because as women we have been told it's our "crowning glory." Maybe it's because I like my hair. It's a bit "mouse-y" in color but turns a nice blonde in the sun (so I don't have to color it!) and it's thick. Okay, so it's not "Farrah Fawcett" hair, but it's fine. And it's mine! And losing it doesn't thrill me. My hair-challenged husband (okay, bald husband) has tried to make me feel better, "we'll be Twinsies!" Family and friends have already tried to tease me with a few wig jokes. But, you know what, I am just not ready for that yet. (God bless anyone who as been through a cancer diagnosis. You must face so many realities and decisions so quickly! Two weeks ago I was innocently enjoying my weekend, worried about how I would keep busy when our daughter left for school, and now, just two weeks later I have cancer, I am having surgery and I am facing CHEMO! It's truly mind-blowing.)

So maybe it's not my fault that the thought of losing my hair makes me sick to my stomach. Maybe I just haven't had enough time to wrap my brain around the fact that losing my hair may save my life. I was in awe as I read an email from my dear friend, Jody. She shared her experience taking "bald" pictures when she was fighting her breast cancer. I am wondering if I can ever be so brave. In front of the mirror as I wash my face at night, I pull back my bangs and wonder, "What will I look like?" and then I cry. Even as I have been talking to my close friends on the phone about it, the thought hasn't gotten any easier.

That is until yesterday. Yesterday Scott and I went to visit with Scotty, my eldest stepson in his new apartment. He has been so supportive already and was asking a lot of questions about my upcoming surgery and treatments. We talked about the possibility of chemo and the subsequent possibility of baldness. Then Scotty told me something that turned my thoughts around. He told me that he and his brothers plan to shave their heads when I lose my hair so that I won't need to feel so self-conscious. He actually said they would do that. I walked out of the apartment with tears in my eyes, thinking for the first time that maybe this won't be SO bad. There's strength in numbers.

> *"It is not in numbers, but in unity that our great strength lies."*   Thomas Paine

The Allen Boys "bald-ready"–Mike, Tom, Scott(Dad) and Scotty

Postcard 8
Plan For The Worst, Hope For The Best

Tuesday, March 9, 2010, 2:36 p.m.

So surgery is tomorrow. Following my "itinerary," I report at 7 a.m. to the Scripps Green Hospital in La Jolla. I have a procedure scheduled at 8 a.m. in which they attach a wire to the tumor which will protrude from the skin. Secretly Scott and I think that it's just so they make sure they operate on the correct side. The "girls" are precious. Let's get this right! Later at 10 a.m I go in for the lumpectomy. During the surgery they will be doing a sentinel node biopsy, which will check my lymph nodes for cancer cells. If all is clear, they close the incisions and I am back at home by mid-afternoon. If they find cancer in the lymph nodes, they will have to remove a greater portion of tissue under my right arm, including nodes. In that case, I will be spending the night. My surgeon recommended I pack a bag "just in case," and as I packed it today I realized I was planning for the worst and but hoping for the best. I ask your continued prayers that the lymph nodes are clear and all goes well. I can't tell you how much it means to both myself and Scott that you are keeping us in your thoughts and prayers. Surrounded and uplifted by prayer we have peace for tomorrow.

Don't worry about anything; instead, pray about everything; tell God your needs and don't forget to thank Him for His answers. If you do this you will experience God's peace, which is far more wonderful than the human mind can understand. His peace will keep your thoughts and your hearts quiet and at rest as you trust in Christ Jesus. Philippians 4:6-7 The Living Bible

Postcard 9
It's Out! Let The Nursing Begin

Wednesday, March 10, 2010, 2:36 p.m.

(Guest post from Pink Warrior's Partner, Scott aka "The Rock")

Great news. Jan did really well in surgery, the tumor is gone and the tests in the lymph system were negative! The news couldn't be any better. So for the next few days, I get to be in charge. Communication will be at a minimum as I have already turned off her phone and have forbid her from writing so she can recover. We will be in peace and quiet so she can rest.

Thank you all for your love and support. It's pretty amazing to see her joy in sharing her journey with you. You will, no doubt, be a key part of her healing but now it's time for a Percocet, some ice packs and a movie. The Percocet is for HER!

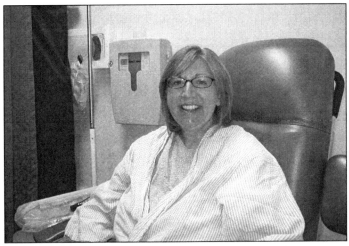

Pink Warrior Prepped for Tumor Removal

Postcard 10
Never Been Hit By A Truck Before

Thursday, March 11, 2010, 4:34 p.m.

I've been blessed never to have had surgery before (except for the joyous day that my son, Zack was born via C-section). I can only imagine what it feels like to be hit by a truck, but I am thinking this is pretty much it! Thankfully, Scott is a wonderful nurse and he makes some amazing homemade Chicken Soup too! I enjoyed a quiet day and watched some good movies. (A little George Clooney is always good for woman's soul.)

Nurse Scott has kept me comfortable with icepacks, cold water, good entertainment, comfort food, and warm blankets and a pain killer every now and then. I have been banned from my cell phone, mainly because my throat is so sore from the breathing tube inserted during surgery. Hopefully I will get phone privileges back tomorrow, but until then I am satisfied with a little written communication. My lymph nodes being clear was an amazing piece of news and I couldn't be more thankful.

This quote has helped me over the past few days and I hope it comforts you today in whatever trial you are facing:

> *"God has not promised sun without rain, joy without sorrow, peace without pain. But God has promised strength for the day, rest for the labor, light for the way, grace for the trials, help from above, unfailing sympathy, undying love."*
>
> Annie Johnson Flint

Cancer-free! Day 1

Postcard 11
Modesty, "Shmodesty"

Friday, March 12, 2010, 8:18 p.m.

Well, I feel much better physically today than I did yesterday! That's a good thing. I even got out for a little fresh air. Today was an appointment I wasn't really looking forward to with the medical oncologist, aka "chemo doctor." But I was hoping to get some answers.

Some women might need the appointment we had today... that gentle awakening that you are now in the place you NEVER dreamed you'd be, "Oncology." You walk in the office, the nurse looks you in the eye and says, "You are in good hands." You can't believe you are here. Seriously. Myself, I think I could have done without this appointment.

Basically, here's the gist of the appointment: 1) you had cancer, we took it out, 2) random cancer cells are more than likely floating around your body, 3) we are going to try to figure out what we can do to prevent those random cells from re-establishing themselves and causing your cancer to recur. Well, isn't that wonderful. Hello? Keeping the cancer away? That sounds like a fabulous idea! Other than that mildly disturbing information, the onc couldn't really tell us anything today. We have to wait.

Wait until the pathology comes back from the tumor. Wait until we see if the "margins are clear." Wait until we see exactly the size of the tumor. Wait until we see if the lymph nodes are clear. Wait. What?? I thought my lymph nodes were clear!?! Well, not exactly—during the surgery they look at the nodes under a microscope but apparently this week they look at the nodes under a bigger, clearer, more precise microscope to see if there really were any cancer cells in them... (okay, as the doctor is telling me this, I am thinking, "hey, they told me in the ultrasound that my nodes looked good, they told me after my surgery and the sentinel node biopsy that my nodes were clear, but now I may still hear, "whoops, they really aren't clear.") But Dr. K, my oncologist, is reassuring. She is encouraged that my cancer has estrogen positive receptors. She is supportive in my choice of a lumpectomy and gives me hope of a complete cure. She doesn't have a lot of answers... yet. But we will get them. We'll meet again next Friday with more information so we can make good decisions. She talked about a test called an Oncotype DX test which I am apparently a "good candidate" for. This test helps determine the benefits of chemotherapy on my specific tumor. I'll have to read up on this.

Even though today's office visit was a bit overwhelming and slightly frustrating Scott and I had a good laugh. After the height, weight and blood pressure, the nurse gives the instructions I've already learned to expect. "Undress from the waist up and the robe opens in the front." Still sore from surgery, Scott helps me off with my jacket, blouse and bra. As we wait for the medical "fellow" (a male) to come in before my "real," official oncologist Dr. K, imagine my horror as I look on the counter and see that Scott has put my bra right on top of my pile of clothes! Oh my gosh! I panic and tell Scott, "Grab my bra and put it under my jacket!"

And then I realize just how incredibly silly that was! I mean my breast still has my surgeon's signature on it! (By the way, we learned that is how they make sure they operate on the correct breast. The surgeon signs the one he is going to work on before the patient goes in to surgery.) It's not like these doctors don't get to check out the "girls." In fact, in the last few weeks I have let at least a dozen health care professionals look at my breasts, like they were looking at my knee or my wrist or any other "public" body part! And, in case there was any question in your mind, yes, I was the girl that dreaded changing in front of the other girls in gym class. But now? "Robe open to the front!" No problem! Modesty, "shmodesty!"

> *Be glad for all God is planning for you. Be patient*
> *in trouble, and prayerful always.*
> Romans 12:12 The Living Bible

Postcard 12
My Heart Is Full.

Sunday, March 14, 2010, 11:01 p.m.

Today was one of those gorgeous southern California days where words can't describe how much I love living here. My sister, Carol, and her daughter, my niece Sonya, flew in yesterday from the midwest, just in time to say goodbye to Scott as he headed for Chicago for work. Carol hasn't been to California since the '80s so we didn't waste any time getting outside.

After church we drove up to Mt. Soledad, a veteran's memorial on the top of a hill with spectacular views. Next we drove out to La Jolla Cove to see the seals and take in some ocean air. After that we drove up to Carlsbad to view the lovely flower fields. The sunshine and ocean breezes were good for the soul. Physically, I'm a bit slow and my body is tired, but family and fresh air has refreshed me. Today I forgot, for a moment, about the cancer.

We spent much of the day remembering my sweet Aunt Gladys who went home to heaven yesterday. She was 97 years young and an inspiration to everyone she met. I am so thankful she was a part of my life and my family for so long—a constant, in this ever-changing world. We will miss her dearly, but I am so happy for her as I know she is reuniting with her husband, sweet Wilmer, and her sisters, my mom Eileen and little Ruth who died as a child. I am grateful that my children had the privilege of knowing and loving Aunt Gladys and I only hope that I can bring honor to her memory in my life. I am so blessed by the wonderful women in my family.

"A sister is a gift to the heart, a friend to the spirit,
a golden thread to the meaning of life."

Isadora James

Jan and her Aunt Gladys, September 2009

Sonya (niece), Jan and Carol (sister) near the Carlsbad flower fields

Postcard 13
Returning To The Scene Of The Crime

Wednesday, March 17, 2010, 12:10 a.m.

So today I had my "post op" visit with my surgeon. First off, let me share the good news (GREAT news!) My lymph nodes were CLEAR, even under the microscope! Yay! And they actually took 4 nodes, 2 "sentinel" nodes and 2 incidental nodes and all were A-Ok!

Now for the less thrilling but and a bit unexpected report— the tumor was a bit larger than anticipated. It was 2.6 cm x 2.1 cm x 1.5 cm. Not exactly pork chop size but anything over 2 cm puts me into Stage ll cancer, but that is still early and still very treatable. And then a bit more less than thrilling news— the surgeon must "return to the scene of the crime." One of the four margins when they removed the tumor was close but not clear. It was only a 0.6mm margin, not big enough, so he's going back in. Next week, I will have an outpatient procedure to re-open the incision and remove a bit more tissue. To explain, (and I will reference the fabulous book a dear friend gave me, *Breast Cancer, Real Questions, Real Answers* by Dr. David Chan) the lumpectomy tissue removed is ideally the entire tumor and a "margin" of clean breast tissue surrounding it. After the surgery, the lab slices the tumor into sections that look like cross sections of an orange. The idea is that in each section you will have a narrow area (similar to the peel which surrounds an orange) that will surround the cancerous tissue. In my case, one of the sections had a VERY thin "peel" of 0.6mm and my oncology team doesn't think that is sufficient to ensure that they got it all. (They want it to be 2-3 mm).

So stay tuned — further evidence will be revealed in the case of the Pink Warrior vs. the Carcinoma, when we return to the scene of the crime!

Postcard 14
Celebration Of A Sweet Life

Friday, March 19, 2010 9:00 p.m.

Currently, I am in my little hometown of New Haven, Indiana for my Aunt Gladys' funeral. I am glad she never had to know that I had this disease. Her daughter Ruth and I made the conscious decision not to tell her because I know she would have worried. Now she is heaven with my mom and their presence in heaven together comforts me. The funeral was a wonderful celebration of her life. It was an emotional boost, though physically draining, to see so many of my family who I haven't seen in a long time. My brothers and sister and I are together down on the farm for the first time in a long time. Their love and support is incredibly uplifting.

> *"Rejoice with your family in the beautiful land of life!"*
> Albert Einstein

Family down on the Farm! Carol (sister), Paul (brother), Jan, Gene (brother), and Ruth (cousin)

Postcard 15
Do I Really Want to Know? And Why Didn't Anyone Tell Me That Earlier?

Monday, March 22, 2010, 4:17 p.m.

Today I am back in southern California and it was time for the second visit to the medical oncologist (chemo czar). She had the results from the pathology of the tumor that was removed during the lumpectomy and was beaming with the "good news!" Her joy was evident as she shared with me the the lymph nodes were negative.

Thrilled as I was upon hearing this news last week, I guess I hadn't grasped the weight of this result. "A cancer with no lymph node involvement is usually easier to treat and has a better outlook for survival." *(Source: American Cancer Society.)* Dr. K went on to recommend the Oncotype DX test I referred to before in a previous postcard. The test is applicable for pre-menopausal women who have cancer with estrogen positive receptors and no lymph node involvement. That's me! This test is done at the Genomic Health Clinical Laboratory in California on the tissue of the tumor to determine the recurrence rate of my particular cancer. They are shipping off a piece of my nasty lesion as I write this, so they can do the test.

But, I ask myself quietly, "Do I really want to know?" There are 3 outcomes possible: 1) a high number—this means my cancer would have a high chance of coming back and chemo treatments would be a definite recommendation; 2) a low number—this means my cancer would have a small likelihood of recurring and chemo treatments would be not so beneficial and therefore not recommended; 3) an intermediate number—this means that my cancer may or may not return, but because of my age, my doctor would rather be on the safe side and she would still recommend chemo. Now, Dr. K made it VERY clear that whatever the outcome of the test, the decision to do chemo treatments is ours alone. It is nice to be able to make the call, but I trust the experts and I do want to do whatever is necessary. I am grateful that there is such a test, but in the back of my mind, I know I don't want the result to be a high number, no matter what.

While we were at the cancer center we scheduled the "clear the margins" surgery for Wednesday. The surgeon will use the existing incision and no other should be necessary.

Ending today's post on a positive note, as we left Dr. K's office, she reiterated the good news—clear lymph nodes, the cancer is "localized." And though Scott and I had been encouraged by this, we didn't actually know the significance of this until as she walked out the door, she said, "clear lymph nodes, the most important factor in a complete cure rate." (See Appendix A) Now why didn't anyone tell me that earlier?

> *I will praise the Lord no matter what happens. I will constantly speak of His glories and grace. I will boast of all His kindness to me. Let all who are discouraged take heart. Let us praise the Lord together and exalt His name.*
>
> Psalm 34:1-3 The Living Bible Translation

Postcard 16

New Weapon Unveiled In Battle Of Pink Warrior VS. The Carcinoma!

Tuesday, March 23, 2010, 10:19 a.m.

Though that Oncotype DX test could seriously prove extremely valuable, I am talking about something else that has proven key to this warrior's comfort—SHEEPIE!!!

And she is an unlikely hero, but a hero nonetheless!

A few years ago my children, Zack and Savannah, gave me "sheepie" for Christmas. She remains right by my bedside each day and night, and is faithful to comfort me when I am missing my kiddos (which is often, since we spend a lot of time apart across the country.) Over the last few days since I am still recovering from the surgery which removed several lymph nodes, my armpit has become very painful! It feels just like a big rug burn under the arm but when you look in the mirror the skin looks normal. Last night, I was searching for something to give me relief when I remembered a friend had a similar operation and a similar problem. She used a small pillow to ease the discomfort. Enter "Sheepie!" I placed her under my arm last night and "ahhhhhhhhh!" It was amazing the difference she made. I have been keeping her close ever since: however, I think she may look silly today when I go to work! I guess she will probably have to stay in the car.

SHEEPIE!

Postcard 17

Does A Chocolate Shake Qualify As A "Clear Liquid?" Of Course!

Wednesday, March 24, 2010, 6:45 p.m.

Fortunately for me, Round 2 of surgery was done at the Rancho Bernardo Scripps Clinic, not the Scripps Green Hospital Complex where I had my lumpectomy. Why was this so fortunate? Because there was an "In-N-Out Burger" across the street! Just minutes after discharge following the procedure, I had an "In-N-Out" CHOCOLATE Shake in my hand! Okay, so it wasn't the "clear liquids" the nurse recommended but I managed to "force" it down.

Everything went well during the procedure. My surgeon assured Scott that he cleared the margins today and that my recovery should be much easier this time around, since there was no incision for the lymph nodes. As a testimony to this, I already feel much better than last time, even able to write on my own. I do have one lousy headache this time, but other than that nothing a little ice and a little pain killer can't cure. Nurse Scott is standing by and Sheepie is doing her job under my arm.

"Don't wreck a sublime chocolate experience by feeling guilty."   Lora Brody

Postcard 18
"Let's Talk Chemo!"

Friday, March 26, 2010, 10:20 a.m.

So this is now my life. I attended a mandatory class yesterday afternoon at the hospital to prepare for the prospect of chemotherapy. The class was called, "Let's Talk Chemo!" (I am sure that catchy name gets so many to sign up.)

I told Nurse Scott that he could take a pass on this one, just too depressing (plus he had some big meetings at work) so I dragged my dear friend Kim along. She was such a good sport. It takes a lot of "hutzpah" to even walk in to the "Cancer Center." They are always cheerful and greeted us promptly. They even offered us a bouquet of fresh daffodils—"Daffodils for Hope." A nice touch, but not enough to make us feel better about announcing ourselves as attendees to the "Let's Talk Chemo!" class. Just something about that makes me laugh. Did I ever dream a few weeks ago that I would be here?! Absolutely not.

I won't bore you with the details of the class where we went over details of pre-meds, post-meds, side effects including hair loss and mouth sores. We even covered a "laxative protocol!" Unbelievable. Then we took a walk up to the 3rd floor to the chemo treatment room. All I can say is that it was so sad. All 4 beds and 2 chairs were full. The patients looked tired and stone faced, old and alone.

It makes me sad that day after day people are going to chemo and dealing with cancer issues and I have just been going on with my life not even giving it a thought. I have never had a glimpse into this walk of life. I have had a few friends who have had cancer and I certainly never got involved at all with what they were truly going through. I am sorry I didn't. Part of what I am learning on this journey is about compassion (or rather, my lack of compassion.) When I met Scott, he had a large wallhanging at his house which was engraved with the Serenity Prayer and it is food for thought for today:

"God grant me the serenity to accept the things
I cannot change; courage to change the things I
can; and wisdom to know the difference."
Reinhold Niebuhr

Postcard 19
March Madness

Saturday, March 27, 2010, 8:28 p.m.

It's the weekend! I am so glad it is only Saturday and I have another day of "rest!" One of the things that has really surprised me over the last few weeks is how "up and down" I feel. I might feel great for an hour or two and then I feel exhausted again. I know a lot of it is physical, but I also think a lot of it is emotional. Today I fell asleep on the couch (for my *second* nap of the day...yikes!) during some March Madness matchup. I woke up several hours later and I thought it was still the same game and was sure I hadn't slept too long. I guess this is what they call "fatigue." I've never been a real basketball fan, and I am quite sure I am a disappointment to my Indiana heritage.

I was snoozing in my normal corner of the couch. This corner has been converted to "Jan's convenience corner." I am completely set up with my laptop, cell phone, pillows, magazines, books, "Sheepie!," pills and prunes (definitely will come in handy with the laxative protocol. Ha!) It's actually pretty remarkable the things within arms reach available to entertain me. Still I have to say, staying in the apartment when I am used to being out and about so much has contributed to little bit of my own "March Madness." Tomorrow I will get out and enjoy this beautiful spring!

Postcard 20

"Nothing is Quite as Funny as the Unintended Humor of Reality"–Steve Allen

Sunday, March 28, 2010, 6:06 p.m.

Say that again? "Nothing is quite as funny as the unintended humor of reality." I read that quote from Steve Allen last night in *Chicken Soup for the Survivor's Soul*. My copy is much loved and well-worn, gifted to me from my dear friend Jody, a breast cancer survivor. I have thoroughly enjoyed the anecdotes in the book and that quote in particular struck me as truth today.

When I left you yesterday you knew I planned to head outside today to enjoy this beautiful Southern California spring! We have had incredible warm temps and sunny skies. Scott and I decided to take our Audi TT convertible to Palm Sunday service, top down. The sunshine and fresh air felt amazing! In fact, I was feeling great after church so we decided to head north I-15 to see what we could find and what trouble we could get into. The TT goes fast and Scott was weaving in and out of traffic. The scenery was gorgeous, snow on the mountaintops before us as we enjoyed 80 degree temps in the valley below. Of course I wouldn't miss a chance to snap a few "selfies."

I have shared with you that I am having a hard time coming to terms with possible hair loss from chemo, right? Well, after I snapped a few photos of us, the idea came to me that maybe being bald would be an improvement when enjoying the convertible.

"In order to laugh, you must be able to play with your pain."   Annette Goodheart

"Nothing is quite as funny as the unintended humor of reality"–
Steve Allen

Postcard 21
Storm Or Sunshine? What Do I Need?

Wednesday, March 31, 2010, 11:46 a.m.

On Tuesday I will find out the results of the Oncotype DX test. The Oncotype DX test is the test that helps to determine if chemo is beneficial by testing the tumor tissue. Several people have asked me this week what to pray for and the truth is, I am not sure what to tell them.

On the one hand, I would love for the test result number to come in really, really low. This would indicate that the cancer has a small chance of recurring and that chemo would not be that beneficial to me and I could dodge the chemo "bullet!" But on the other hand, I know that I want to do everything I can to kill this cancer here and now to prevent a later recurrence. A higher test result number would indicate that chemo treatment would be beneficial; it would help. And as much as I am griping about hair loss and the other side effects of chemo treatment, goodness knows I want to do whatever I can now to stop the growth of cancer cells inside my body. I play both scenarios over and over in my brain. It's all a part of this disturbing cancer "numbers game." This little analogy from *Streams in the Desert* by L.B. Cowman spoke to me today:

> *"Many years ago there was a monk who needed olive oil, so he planted an olive tree sapling. After he finished planting it, he prayed, "Lord, my tree needs rain so its tender roots may drink and grow. Send gentle showers." And the Lord*

55

sent gentle showers. Then the monk prayed, "Lord, my tree needs sun. Please send it sun." And the sun shone, gilding the once-dripping clouds. "Now send frost, dear Lord, to strengthen its branches," cried the monk. And soon the little tree was covered in sparkling frost, but by evening it had died.

Then the monk sought out a brother monk in his cell and told him of his strange experience. After hearing the story, the other monk said, "I also have planted a little tree. See how it is thriving! But I entrust my tree to its God. He who made it knows better than a man like me what it needs. I gave God no constraints or conditions, except to pray, 'Lord, send what it needs— whether that be a storm or sunshine, wind, rain, or frost. You made it and you know best what it needs.'"

Postcard 22
"Good" Friday?

Good Friday, April 2, 2010, 10:27 p.m.

When I was a little girl, I remember every year asking my mother, "Why is today "Good" Friday?" Because, really, it didn't seem any better than any other Friday. I mean we always had to go to this really scary church service where the pastor screamed all the words that Jesus said from the cross and my cousin Ruth always sang "Were You There?" (which was a really sad song). And my mother's answer to me was always, "Today is Good Friday because today is day that Jesus died for us." Again, sad. Not really "good."

As a child, after that rather disturbing church service we always went directly to my Aunt Gladys' home to color Easter eggs. That was good! And a ton of fun. Fond memories I will carry with me forever. She always made a "lunch" afterwards, which was really more like a meal. As a kid, that's what made Good Friday, good.

Now, as an adult, I have been reflecting on the meaning of "Good" Friday. I am beginning to understand that the day that Jesus died on the cross was really the day that God showed us how to love, how to be "good."

That same cousin Ruth, who sang a solo each Good Friday, gave me a bracelet for Christmas this year that was inscribed with the words of John 3:16: "For God so loved the world that He gave His only Son, that whosoever believes in Him should not perish, but have eternal life." While I was at my Aunt Gladys' funeral a few weeks ago, I found out that same verse was her confirmation (or first communion) verse (in German of course). Coincidence? Maybe. Maybe not. Maybe God is trying to tell me something. The verse says that God so LOVED us that He sacrificed His Son for us, and the day we celebrate that is "Good" Friday. His death means love, sacrificial love. Truly that IS love, when you make a sacrifice for someone else.

I hope that you all have felt that kind of love. I have. I have experienced that love from Zack and Savannah last June when they put all their funds together so they could buy me a TomTom navigation system for my birthday. That was a lot of money for two young teenagers, but they gave it gladly to surprise me with something I had really wanted. And Scott has been making sacrifices for me daily since I met him, but especially since we have received the cancer diagnosis. He has never wavered, no matter how busy or tired he is, to make sure I am okay and taken care of, or that I have his hand to hold at each doctor's appointment. Many of my friends and family have made sacrifices for me over the past month and I am eternally grateful.

Those precious sacrifices—calling or emailing me, writing a card, saying a prayer, cooking a meal, making a bracelet, sending a package or flowers—mean the world to this Pink Warrior. Love that makes sacrifices, that puts the other person first is powerful, it is committed, it is honest and genuine, it is GOOD.

So maybe I am finally able to grasp what is so good about Good Friday. It is God's example of love.

Happy Easter!

Postcard 23

"Former Flight Attendant returns to airport again, and again, and again, and yet again!"

Wednesday, April 7, 2010, 11:45 p.m.

Wow! Today was a crazy day. The last time I visited the airport this many times in one day was when I was a flight attendant on the Pan Am Shuttle and flew every hour on the hour between LaGuardia and Boston! Early this morning I dropped my niece off at San Diego airport after a wonderful Easter visit. Then, for Round 2, I took my kids, Zack and Savannah, back to that same airport just before noon to catch their flight to Chicago and then ultimately ending up in Columbus, Ohio. They were delayed 3 hours on the tarmac for weather in Chicago, but navigated O'Hare like the professional world travelers they are (at age 17 and 13). They made their connection to Columbus as the gate agent was announcing, "Last call for Zachary and Savannah, party of 2." A few hours later I had to return once again to San Diego airport to head to San Jose. This weekend I am working the Pebble Beach Food and Wine Festival where my company is a sponsor. In conjunction with our sponsorship, I am bringing in a chef from Aruba and Chef Miguel arrived a couple hours after I did into San Jose International, so I returned to the airport once again to fetch him and take him back to his hotel. Whew!!!

After all that travel today, my pillow is calling my name, but I didn't want to fall asleep tonight without giving you an update on my status. Yesterday's appointment with the chemo doctor was cancelled. This was the appointment where we were supposed to find out the results of the Oncotype DX test. Unfortunately the lab has not processed the results yet and so there was no reason to hold the appointment. As soon as the results come in, I will schedule an appointment. Just another chapter in this waiting game. On a happy note, I have been kept busy preparing for a life "sans" hair! Details coming soon about a Fabulous Fashion Show featuring the latest in Hat Couture as well as my afternoon at the wig shop!

Workin' it at the Pebble Beach Food and Wine Festival

Postcard 24
Heaven At The Hyatt

Monday, April 12, 2010, 7:27 p.m.

It's been almost a week since my last post. I have been busy working hard at the Pebble Beach Food and Wine Festival in Northern California. Our chef, Miguel Garcia did an incredible job as we hosted a booth with local island dishes and information on Aruba, "One Happy Island." Scott joined me for the event and was a huge help. We were surrounded by incredible culinary talent including Tyler Florence, Jacques Pepin, Wolfgang Puck, the Iron Chef Morimoto and many more. Keeping up with work as much as I can has certainly kept my mind off of what is really going on with me and my cancer diagnosis.

While we were gone in Pebble Beach, my husband's executive team at Hyatt Regency La Jolla were extremely busy. Today, they called me into their offices. I was surprised and I certainly had no idea I was about to get a glimpse of heaven. My husband and I have lived at Hyatt La Jolla for over 2 years. He is the General Manager and living in the hotel is quite a blessing. The hotel is a gorgeous property in a wonderful neighborhood and we have surely enjoyed our time here; but one of the things we have missed was some outdoor living space. We both enjoy the outdoors and have loved the environment surrounding our former homes. We lived on the beach while on the island of Aruba and had a private wooded lot at our home in Maineville, Ohio. Here in La Jolla, where the weather is gorgeous, Scott and I have missed having our own personal space to relax outdoors and enjoy beautiful Southern California sunshine. My doctors have also encouraged me to get out and breathe some fresh air, relax and soak in some Vitamin D but I have been somewhat self-conscious to go out in my "fatigued" state and mingle at the hotel pool so I have been holed up indoors. Well, not anymore!

The team surprised us by creating a stunning "piece of heaven" on the roof. Yes, I said, ROOF of the hotel! We now have our own oasis featuring 2 lounge chairs with cushions and pillows, magazine rack and comfy blankets, a gas grill, a table for two, refrigerator and soothing fountain on the private rooftop of the property. What more could a girl with cancer ask for? This afternoon we all christened it with champagne. And I couldn't stop the tears. I was so emotionally touched by the oasis that Scott's team had created—a shelter from the "storm" that is our life right now. Along the walls in our little oasis are some wonderful quotes to ponder while relaxing in this quiet haven—"Together — A great place to be," "*Always Rejoice in the Lord*" Philippians 4:4 (The Voice), and "Expect a miracle everyday." This place will be a haven of solitude, peacefulness and inspiration for me as I fight this battle. And I am SO grateful.

Jan and Scott Celebrating the New Rooftop Haven

Postcard 25
Who Is that Cat in the HAT?

Wednesday, April 14, 2010, 10:00 p.m.

Last week my niece Kelly, from Raleigh and her two kids, Grace and Grant, came to visit. Zack and Savannah were home too for their Spring Break. We had tons of fun! In a previous post, I alluded to one of the highlights of the week... actually *the fashion event of the year* here in La Jolla! A fashion show featuring the latest in Hat Couture with the newest young "supermodels," Savannah and Grace. You see Kelly had contacted my family and friends in North Carolina, Ohio, Indiana and even New York and Connecticut and told them about her idea to throw me a "hat shower." So many responded! Some hats were lovingly handmade, some were selected carefully from a cancer website, and others, just gorgeous hats. My cousin, Ruth, even sent a hat that had belonged to my dear Aunt Gladys, knowing she would never have wanted to miss a party! Savannah and Grace took turns modeling hat after hat while Kelly talked them up and down the "runway" in our living room. I laughed so hard, I cried. What a wonderful idea! Here's just a sampling of the hat couture I will be sporting in the coming months:

Savannah (daughter), Kelly (niece), Grace (great-niece)
and photo bomb, Zack (son)

'an't miss the chance to give an update on my doctor
...s: Monday I had BRCA gene testing done. It is a simple blood test that will tell if I carry any genes that indicate hereditary breast cancer. (See Appendix B) I should find out the results in about 2 weeks. Tomorrow I have the medical oncologist appointment where I learn the results of the Oncotype DX test and where we will be planning a treatment plan strategy together with my doctor.

> *"Into all our lives, in many simple, familiar ways, God infuses this element of joy from the surprises of life, which unexpectedly brighten our days, and fill our eyes with light."*
>
> Samuel Longfellow

Postcard 26
Storms in the Forecast...

Thursday, April 15, 2010, 8:24 p.m.

Not your typical San Diego weather forecast, but there is a storm moving in.

"Storms or Sunshine?" was the subject of my post on March 31. Not sure what to pray for at that time, I decided to pray that God would give me whatever I needed. Remember the analogy of the little olive tree sapling?

So it seems perhaps a storm is moving in.

Walking in to the oncologist's office Scott and I knew we were expecting the results of the Oncotype DX test. (The test gives a number that indicates the recurrence factor of my specific cancer after the lab has analyzed my particular tumor. In simple terms, the test result is a number 1 to 100, 1 being a 1% chance the cancer will return in 10 years, a 50 would mean that there is a 50/50 chance the cancer will return in 10 years.) We had decided ahead of time that ONLY if the number was remarkably low would we forego chemo. Our thought was that even if the benefit of chemo was relatively low we would go forward with it, knowing that it may not make a huge difference but that even a small difference was worth it! I don't want the cancer to ever come back. So today going in to the appointment I thought in my mind that the number would be 17. (Not sure why, it was just the number that kept coming into my head.) A low number is desirable, which would mean a low chance of recurrence. Last night on a breastcancer.org online forum I had been reading about some women's similar test results and saw one woman who had a 63. Wow, I thought, "that would really kind of freak me out." So imagine my distress today when my test came back with a result of 71. Yes, that's right, 71! (My premonition of 17 had the digits right, just not in the right order. Bummer.) A 71 isn't good.

It is important to share that my numbers baffled my highly experienced oncologist. Here's why (without getting too technical)—my original pathology report came back after the biopsy during surgery that my cancer was Estrogen Receptor positive (ER+) by 91% and Negative for the Progesterone Receptor and HER2. The ER Positive result was great because that means that the cancer feeds on Estrogen and there are many treatments for that, most common, form of cancer. For example, Tamoxifen (hormone therapy) starves the cancer cells of estrogen and keeps it from coming back. This hormone therapy is a wonderful tool to be able to use to fight the cancer after all other treatments are completed.

But here's the strange thing, the Oncotype test done remotely at a high tech clinical laboratory conflicted with my original pathology done at my surgical center. On the Oncotype DX test we got back today, it showed my tumor as being negative on ALL 3 receptors including the ER Receptor. Triple Negative is bad news. That means that there is no evidence of what the cancer "feeds on" or what causes it to grow. The "receptors" are indications of how the cancer is being fed and growing. A "triple negative" breast cancer gives the physicians treating the disease no clue as to how to stop it or slow it down. Dr. K, my oncologist is puzzled because she said she has NEVER had a case with such a large discrepancy. I mean to show 91% ER+ (estrogen receptor positive) on the original labs and then completely Negative for Estrogen on the Oncotype test has never happened in her practice. To try to make some sense of these results, she is running the test over in the surgical centers pathology lab. To re-run the Oncotype test is virtually impossible because of the high cost of the test (approximately $3500).

In the meantime we have decided to go ahead immediately with chemotherapy. I will have my first treatment next week. The good news is if I truly am "triple negative" the chemo will be extremely beneficial.

Today at Dr. K's office it became clear that the storm clouds are moving in, but I am not afraid. I know that God is in control and that the storm will pass and it's needed, maybe even welcomed. For now, I am glad I have a wonderful selection of hats to shelter me in the rain.

Postcard 27
Happy Hour on Friday!

Saturday, April 17, 2010, 10:36 a.m.

I just found out that I will have my first chemo treatment Friday at 2 p.m.. Not the kind of cocktail I enjoy on a typical Friday afternoon, but I will still be looking forward to that "Happy Hour." I anticipate a delightful cocktail of Taxotere and Cytoxan. This "happy hour" means I will get started attacking these nasty little cancer cells floating around in my bloodstream. I will definitely be losing my hair, so today Scott and I will go and make the big wig purchase (And I am talking big! Who knew real hair wigs cost nearly $700?) Over Spring Break, I got the approval from my kids and my niece's family on the style, but today I am taking Scott to see if he prefers a red-head or if it's really true that "Gentlemen prefer Blondes."

This morning while lounging in my heavenly oasis on the roof I was reading the daily devotional that I love, "Streams in the Desert" by L.B. Cowman. Today's reading was wonderful and I hope that it may help some of you in whatever you are going through as it helped me.

> *"A number of years ago the most magnificent diamond in the world was discovered in an African mine. It was presented to the king of England to embellish his crown of state. The king sent it to Amsterdam to be cut by an expert stonecutter. He took this gem of priceless value and... struck it one time hard with a hammer and the*

*majestic jewel fell into his hand, brokʳ
What recklessness! What wastefulneˢ*

*Actually that's not the case at all. ...thᵉ
with the hammer had been studied and planⁿⁱᶜ
for days, even weeks. Drawings and models had
been made of the gem... And the man to whom
it was entrusted was one of the most skilled
stonecutters in the world. Now do you believe
that blow was a mistake? No, it was the cap-
stone and culmination of the stonecutter's skill.
When he struck that blow, he did the one thing
that would bring that gem to its most perfect
shape, radiance and splendor. ... The blow that
seemed to be the ruin of the majestic precious
stone was actually its perfect redemption, for
from the halves were fashioned two magnificent
gems. Only the skilled eye of the expert stonecutter could have seen the beauty of two dia-
monds hidden in the rough, uncut stone as it
came from the mine.*

*Sometimes, in the same way God allows a
stinging blow fall on your life. You bleed, feeling
the pain, and your soul cries out in agony. At
first you think the blow is an appalling mistake.
But it is not, for you are the most precious jewel
in the universe to God. And he is the most skilled
stonecutter in the universe.*

Someday you are to be a jewel adorning the crown of the King. As you lie in His hand now, he knows just how to deal with you. Not one blow will be permitted to fall on your apprehensive soul except what the love of God allows. And you may be assured from the depths of this experience, you will see untold blessings, and spiritual enrichment you have never before imagined."

Cheers!

Postcard 28
I Am A Lover, Not A Fighter!

Tuesday, April 20, 2010, 4:59 p.m.

Over the last couple weeks, I have been having a hard time moving myself toward "fighting mode." I am much more of a "lover" personality, and not so much a "fighter." But I know that I have to get myself in a mindset to battle this disease that has invaded my body. Pink *Warrior*, right? And I know the "fight" mentality is important and actually very Biblical. Many scriptures refer to "warriors," i.e. "putting on the full armor of God" (Ephesians 6:10-17). I mentioned to a friend over coffee last week that I was having trouble with the Warrior mentality. Suddenly I remembered that I was a "Warrior" in high school. We were the Woodlan "Warriors." In those "glory days" I was always competing for the prize. I was always a fierce competitor. Not so much in athletics, I have near zero talent there! Truth. But I *did* compete in music and drama competitions and also academically. In fact, like my Aunt Gladys before me, I became the valedictorian of my high school class. I started to ask myself last week what got me to compete back then? Of course, it was always the PRIZE. I like winning. I like being rewarded, who doesn't?

So I guess my husband, Scott, knows me pretty well. Maybe he sensed my lack of inspiration over the last week. He also knows I do much better working toward a goal, and even better if that goal is a reward of some kind. So he set out to find a prize for me, something for me to set my sights on, something beyond the chemo and radiation treatments that

75

would inspire me. We will be celebrating 5 years of wedded bliss next month. (I should be some gorgeous bride by then huh? All puke-y and bald. Yikes.) And I won't be able to take any exotic trips to celebrate. But he found an awesome website called BiddingforGood.com which is an auction website and all the money from the auctions goes to various philanthropic causes. Without my knowledge, he started looking for something special later this year and he found something AMA-ZING. Two VIP tickets to the American Music Awards in November including tickets to the After Party (donated by the American Music Awards with the funds going to the Boys and Girls Clubs in California). Scott was successful with his bidding strategy and we will be attending the AMA's at the Nokia Theatre in Los Angeles on November 21st. Now that's something to look forward to! I LOVE music and can't wait to see who will be performing there. Now I have some motivation to get in fighting shape! With that date in mind for our anniversary celebration, I can begin this fight. And God willing, I may even be sporting a new do with my OWN hair by then! What an incredible "groom" I have!

> *"True love possesses the ability to see beyond. In that sense we might say love has x-ray vision. It goes beyond mere words. It sees beneath the veneer. Love focuses on the soul. Love sees another's soul in great need of help and sets compassion to work."* Charles Swindoll

Postcard 29

"There ain't much fun in medicine, but there's a heck of a lot of medicine in fun." Josh Billings

Thursday, April 22, 2010, 6:49 p.m.

Tomorrow is a new "first" for me. I have had an amazing amount of adventure in my 44 years but tomorrow starts something completely new and a bit overwhelming. Chemotherapy treatment. I am looking at it as Friday afternoon "Happy Hour." A few years ago we were living in Aruba and each week my friend Meredith and I would look forward to "Tranquilo Friday." With those fond memories in mind, I will consider tomorrow my new "Tranquilo Friday" experience! I am ready to go tomorrow with my bag packed for my 3 hour cocktail session; I have music loaded with 2 possible playlists depending on how I feel—"Happy Hour" and "Chillax." My Kindle is in the bag with an exciting mystery novel to delve into and I have a "Soul Soothing Crossword" puzzle book, a couple snacks, a little candy, and my necessary medications. Also, my camera. I never go too far without the camera!

On that note, I thought I could use a few laughs tonight so I've decided to post a few photos taken on my 2 trips to the Wig Shop "Hair Unlimited." The name sounds so promising, doesn't it? In the photos is my own personal angel, Claudia, who made this tedious process easy. Being surrounded by my family made the whole session so much better too. Not gonna lie, as I tried on the first wig the tears almost started flowing but soon the family had me laughing.

"Angel" Claudia, Jan, Grace, Savannah, Grant (great-nephew),
Zack in background

Scott Joins the Fun

"Pink Warrior" in a Pink Wig!

Postcard 30
Just A Verse For Today...

Friday, April 23, 2010, 11:13 a.m.

It is amazing to me how God speaks right to us in so many different ways, maybe through a friend or your pastor or his living word on paper. And even though I am running around like "a chicken with my head cut off" trying to get everything done that I want to get done before "happy hour" later today, I had to share this scripture from my devotion today in "Streams in the Desert":

> *Though I walk in the midst of trouble, You preserve my life.* Psalm 138:7a

The author went on to explain that the literal translation of this verse in Hebrew means to "go on in the center of trouble." With my first chemo session today I guess that is right where I am headed. The nurses in the chemotherapy center will be dripping poison in my veins for 3 hours. If that is not the center of trouble I don't know what is. But I am going right on in, with confidence! I know I am not alone and it is all for my ultimate good. I am ready for that cocktail. Join me in spirit this "happy hour." Cheers to "Tranquilo Friday!"

Postcard 31
The Hangover

Saturday, April 24, 2010, 11:41 a.m.

So what do you expect Saturday morning after "Tranquilo Friday?" A bit of a hangover, I guess, and yesterday's Happy Hour did not disappoint. Here's an update after Chemo Round 1. Yesterday we reported to the Dr's office at 2 p.m. and walked back in the door at home last night at 7:30 p.m. The treatments went very well: 15 min infusion of anti-nausea meds, 1 hour and 15 mins of Cytoxan and 1 hour and 15 mins of Taxotere. I was proud to make it through all without any reactions, though the Taxotere made me feel a bit flush, all went fine and was able to enjoy my "Happy Hour" playlist and read a mindless magazine.

Last night after I got home I felt pretty much like a huge lead balloon. I sank so deep in the mattress and didn't want to move. Just a little bit of nausea and sleeplessness which some meds took care of and I was out like a light. This morning I have to say, I have quite a "hangover." I am fine just sitting still, but moving causes some issues, including dizziness and nausea.

Certainly, I am happy to have 1 treatment down! My attending Nurse Scott is here to help with anything I need. And just now I smell some yummy chicken soup on the stove.

An awesome verse, shared with me today from an awesome friend:

In the multitude of my anxieties within me, Your comforts delight my soul.   Psalm 94:19 NKJV

Postcard 32
It's Working...

Monday, April 26, 2010, 7:23 p.m.

Just a quick note tonight, I am tired.

Over the last couple days since my first chemo treatment, I've been feeling pretty good and it was causing me to question—"is the chemo working?," "when will I start really feeling it?" Most of you know, I truly enjoy baking and I use yeast a lot, especially for my family's favorite, German coffeecake. When I bake with yeast, I start by adding a few tablespoons of yeast with water in a cup (and a little sugar for good measure) and then I wait. Wait until the yeast (hopefully!) expands. I wait with hopeful expectation that I haven't completely killed it with too hot or too cold water (which is easy to do). Nothing happens for a while and then, if the water temperature was right, it seems like all of a sudden it is overflowing the sides of the cup.

Over the weekend, I was feeling a little like yeast... wondering if the medication was working because I didn't feel too much different. Silly me. Today I can say... it's working... "overflowing the sides of the cup."

And I am convinced and sure of this very thing, that He who began a good work in you will continue until the day of Jesus Christ, developing and perfecting and bringing it to full completion in you.   Philippians 1:6 Amplified Bible

Postcard 33
What I Am Thankful For Today

Tuesday, April 27, 2010, 5:47 p.m.

Today I am trying to focus on the positives in my life. I have been thinking about just a few things that I am thankful for:

- a husband who is an excellent cook
- gorgeous, smart kids
- potato gnocchi
- gouda
- new 'under the cabinet' lighting in my kitchen
- working from home
- a hot bath
- caring friends (and family)
- a comfy couch
- medicine (from aspirin to chemo meds)
- music
- text messaging
- English Breakfast tea
- my hair
- my wig
- magazines
- healing
- the remote
- flowers
- an old familiar and friendly wool comforter
- the microwave
- my slippers
- CORN POPS!!!
- feather pillows
- the mail
- makeup
- Bananagrams
- my laptop and the internet
- a warm hug
- photos
- a sweet apple
- the hope of enjoying the roof tomorrow

Give thanks in all circumstances; for this is God's will for you in Christ Jesus.　　　1 Thessalonians 5:18

Postcard 34
I'm "Rash-alicious"

Wednesday, April 28, 2010, 3:02 p.m.

A couple years ago my daughter and I got to see Fergie at the San Diego County Fair. The concert was great and (thanks to Savannah's dad, a Cincinnati radio personality) we had backstage passes and got to meet her! Fergie was so nice to Savannah and even took a couple photos with her and since then we have been big fans. She has a couple hits that have made my playlists, "Big Girls Don't Cry," "Glamorous" and "Fergalicious." These happy songs make me smile, remembering the concert and, much to Savannah's chagrin, bring out my own "inner diva."

Cancer has a way of messing with that "inner diva" mindset, but I am trying to keep a positive spirit. The side effects of the chemo drugs are setting in. I was rejoicing that I may possibly be over the major body aches but, yikes! Imagine my surprise when I looked in the mirror last night and a major rash is climbing down my neck. "Glamorous?" Right? Not so much. I climbed into bed and said to Scott, "Guess what? Major rash." He took one look and said, "That's okay, my girl, you're just 'rash-alicious!'" That's right! I'm "rash-alicious!" And that's not going to squelch the "inner diva" of this Pink Warrior!

"Be happy with what you have and are, be generous with both, and you won't have to hunt for happiness." William E. Gladstone

Postcard 35
Thoughts of Mom

Saturday, May 1, 2010, 6:45 a.m.

My thoughts have been drifting a lot in the last few weeks to my mom. I am not sure if it's because Mother's Day is around the corner, or if my cancer diagnosis has made me long for her, or maybe mourning the loss of my Aunt Gladys has brought to mind memories of happy times.

I lost my mom in February of 1982, as a 16 year old junior in high school. My son is a junior in high school now! Wow. The other night I was wondering, what was my mom's life like at 44? Then I had to laugh. I wasn't even born yet to my mom when she was 44! So she had a lot of surprises coming up in her life yet, and I am sure I do too! This week I have been pretty brief in my postcards after Chemo Round 1.

My mom ALWAYS said, "if you don't have anything good to say, don't say anything!" Subconsciously, her words echoed in my mind as I contemplated writing this week. Truthfully, there isn't a ton of good news to report. I am more "rash-alicious" than ever! But I do feel like I am past the worst of the side effects. For me, the toughest part was the aching legs that kept me up at night. They were just another reminder of my mom. If you had known her years ago, you would probably remember that she always suffered from aching legs. I think she had "restless leg syndrome" but back then, that was unheard of and not diagnosed. I feel bad now for what I know must have really bothered her and wish there would have been medication for her like there is for me today.

Another trigger to my nostalgic thoughts is the impending spring. Spring always brings thoughts of my mother's gardens. She would begin by planting lettuce on Good Friday in a patch by the kitchen window and then expand her efforts across our farm. By fall, the huge vegetable garden behind the house was out of control. Literally! We canned and froze many fruits and vegetables every year that would feed us through the winter, but that garden always had a quite a few weeds that had gotten out of control too. Thinking back, I think the weeding was probably my job and why they got out of control. But my mother's pride and joy year after year, was her flower garden in the front of the house. This garden had rows and rows of various flowers, marigolds, petunias, dusty miller, begonias, zinnias and never a weed! The flowers for my sister's wedding came from that flower bed. And it was always stunning! Near the house my mom had some succulents which she called "Hens and Chicks," a large bloom-shaped cacti surrounded by similar tiny "blooms." I was so delighted to see those same "Hens and Chicks" planted in the flower boxes in my haven on the roof!

So many thoughts of mom in this Mother's Day season. For many seasons now, she has been tending God's gardens. But I know she is full of joy that her daughter is surrounded by the love of so many "moms" here on earth. I am SO grateful for the many women in my life who encourage me daily in so many ways. The encouragement I feel in this fight against breast cancer, in the raising of my children and tending my own "garden" in life, on being a loving wife and dealing with the stresses of each day means so much. Sending notes, cards and listening when I need to talk and offering advice when I need to listen is so precious to me. I am blessed.

"Gratitude consists in a watchful, minute attention to the particulars of our state, and to the multitude of God's gifts, taken one by one. It fills us with a consciousness that God loves and cares for us, even to the least event and smallest need of life."   Henry Edward Manning

Jan (circa 1968) beside her mom's flower bed

Jan and her mom Eileen (circa 1967)

Postcard 36
The Pink Plagues

Tuesday, May 4, 2010, 2:49 p.m.

I don't know how many of you are familiar with the plagues that God sent on the Egyptians centuries ago. Pharaoh, the leader of the Egyptians, would not release God's people, the Israelites, from slavery. Moses and his buddy Aaron kept trying to tell Pharaoh that he needed to let them leave Egypt but he just wouldn't do it. I guess God lost patience with Pharaoh and started to send a series of 10 plagues on the Egyptians which were increasingly more miserable until Pharaoh had had enough and he released all the Israelites and sent them away, even giving them many of the riches of the land.

The plagues were rough. God turned the Nile river to blood. He sent a plethora of frogs, gnats, locusts and flies. He caused their livestock to die and caused boils to form on the Egyptians. He sent hail, 3 days of darkness and even the death of their firstborn sons.

Now I know the analogy is not quite perfect because I don't believe that God is punishing me, but I just had to share that these chemo side effects have a lot of similarities to the plagues. They just keep coming and they are miserable. I have dubbed these side effects the "Pink Plagues." I want to let you know that I have been debating writing this post for a couple days because I don't want my posts to be misconstrued as complaining.

I am not complaining.

I know that all these things must happen so that the chemo medicine can do it's job. And trust me, if the effects on me are any indication, it is doing it's job! I wanted to write this simply to share what it's like, how I am feeling and what's really going on with me. I am doing better than I expected 10 days out from Round 1, but here are a few of the "plagues" I have been dealing with in the last 10 days: 1) Nausea, 2) Bone Pain, 3) "Restless Leg," 4) Constipation, 5) Rash, 6) Dry Mouth, 7) Drippy Nose, 8) Diarrhea, 9) Fatigue, and the 10th I am still looking forward to... 10) Hair Loss (which should be starting any time now). It is such a deep comfort that I have not been alone through all this.

I know that God is right here with me and He is in all the nitty gritty details of dealing with all these crazy "plagues." I am so grateful that He has provided me such an amazing helper in my husband. Scott has been incredibly above and beyond all I had ever imagined as my "rock." And all the kind words, thoughts and deeds from friends are keeping me strong. As I contemplate my own battle, I feel bad that I had no idea what several of my friends who have battled cancer have been through. I could have been a better friend when they were going through this. I pray that as I go through this season of my life my love and compassion for others grows.

Is your life full of difficulties and temptations? Then be happy, for when the way is rough, your patience has a chance to grow. So let it grow, and don't try to squirm out of your problems. For when your patience is finally in full bloom, then you will be ready for anything, strong in character, full and complete. James 1:2-4 The Living Bible

Postcard 37

Top Ten List

Wednesday, May 5, 2010, 4:50 p.m.

Today I am halfway through my week of "quarantine." I am staying inside this week because during days 7-14 my risk of infection is high due to low blood counts. I figure it's not worth it. I don't want to go out, catch some crazy bug and get sick which would delay my treatments. Trying to maintain a positive attitude, I considered the top ten reasons why I enjoy being "cooped up" in our home at the hotel. In the style of one of my favorite late night hosts, David Letterman, here is my Top Ten List for "Why I Am Loving My Self-Induced Quarantine":

Number 10–I can watch unlimited chick flicks!
Number 9–I am aware of breaking news as it breaks.
Number 8–All the office work I put off for sales calls is now getting done.
Number 7–The check book is perpetually balanced.
Number 6–My pile of unread magazines is shrinking.
Number 5–All those "random" items floating around my computer are now in file folders.
Number 4–Going to the roof, doesn't count as "going out."
Number 3–ROOM SERVICE!
Number 2–I am available to Skype at any time, with anyone.
and the Number 1 Reason why it is so awesome being quarantined to our home in the hotel is....

I still have the SAME $20 bill in my wallet that I had last week! (I haven't mentioned to Scott that I have opened up 3 new online shopping accounts!)

Postcard 38
Never Underestimate The Healing Power
Of Ice Cream

Friday, May 7, 2010, 4:55 p.m.

For the last week, I have had a terrible sore throat. I may seem crazy but I think my sore throat is coming from my drippy nose which is coming from the loss of my nose hairs which causes the fluids from my nose to just drip! This chain reaction is not going to be pretty. I am fairly confident that the sore throat is what is driving me to eat ICE CREAM. And I am fairly confident that eating ice cream 3 times a day will lead to weight gain. Arghhh.

The dry mouth and metallic taste in my mouth has ruined the enjoyment of such pleasures as french fries and macaroni and cheese. Those treats taste so salty I don't even want to eat them. (Cancer treatment, specifically chemotherapy can affect your sense of taste. Food may seem to lack flavor or taste too sweet, salty or metallic. Source: Mayo Clinic.) So for a couple of days I thought, "wow, I may actually lose a few pounds." Then a day or two later when I had my first Arby's Jamocha shake in years, I was hooked. I had a Jamocha shake for lunch, a Haagen Daz ice cream bar (there's NO calories in those, right?) for an afternoon snack and a chocolate sundae for dessert after dinner. Delicious! All that ice cream made me feel so much better! I need it!!! It is quickly becoming an addiction.

And I must confess, when I did leave the house for a few minutes this week to drop some mail at the post office, on the way home I couldn't resist. I had to swing through the McDonald's drive-thru for, what else but a large chocolate shake? My hopes were dashed though, after I waited in a long line to order, the speaker said, "I am sorry, we don't have any shakes right now." Bummer. But never fear, soon a blender appeared on my kitchen counter and I was in business! Thankfully, Crystal, a dear friend and cancer survivor, heard of my obsession and has rescued me from myself. She bought me a "smoothie" recipe book. All the cold, creamy, soothing flavor, half the calories! Frozen strawberries, kiwi, honey and yogurt make a perfect pink smoothie to power up this Pink Warrior!

> *Your unfailing love is better to me than life itself;*
> *how I praise you! I will honor you as long as you*
> *live,... you satisfy me more than the richest of*
> *foods. I will praise you with songs of joy!*
> Psalm 63:3-5 NLT

Postcard 39
There is a Time for Everything...

Tuesday, May 11, 2010, 4:45 p.m.

Ecclesiastes 3 (which is the subject of a great song by the Byrds "Turn, Turn, Turn") says "There is a time for everything, a season for every activity under heaven, ... a time to cry and a time to laugh, a time to grieve and a time to dance... a time to search and a time to lose, a time to tear and a time to mend..." A time to have hair and a time to be bald... (my words) I guess, now is my time to be bald. Well, not quite bald. I am sporting a buzz cut. Scott used his skills with a "number 2" last night and this morning I woke up to reality.

Over the last few days, my hair started coming out in handfuls. Yesterday when Scott came home from work my shirt was covered in my long hairs even though I had worn a cap all day. I decided, "what's the point in keeping my hair, when I have to wear a cap to cover the balding spots and to keep the falling hair out of whatever I am working on? Might as well cut it off." Though this is the thing I was most dreading about having cancer and chemo, I have also gained some perspective. In the shower the other day, as I shampooed my hair and it was coming out like crazy, the radio station I was listening to ran a commercial. It was a commercial supporting disabled veterans, and the thought came to me, "At least I am losing my hair, not my leg." And that is my reality. My hair will grow back. Probably different. Maybe gray. But it will grow back eventually. I think what is really bothering me is when I look in the mirror, I think I look sick. I think people may pity me. I don't want that. And actually this week I feel great!

This afternoon I am busy making cupcakes for a women's group I attend. It was really the cupcake-making that got me motivated to shave my hair last night. I certainly didn't want all my hair falling into the batter or the frosting today! The actual shaving wasn't all that bad, though I admit I shed a few tears. My sweet niece Kelly sent me a bottle of "Bald Head Red," a delicious red wine made on Bald Head Island in North Carolina where she lives, and so we uncorked that and went for it. Scott has skills!

"Twinsies!"

Postcard 40
Full Circle

Friday, May 14, 2010, 4:01 p.m.

I was incredibly blessed by family this Mother's Day, especially my "Hyatt Family!" Each year on Mother's Day, the Hyatt sponsors a team that walks a 5k at Mission Bay to benefit "Breast Cancer, Network of Strength." Two years ago, right after moving to San Diego, Scott and I joined this group for a morning of fun and fellowship for a good cause. The organization was established to ensure that no person with breast cancer would ever face the disease alone! Who knew back then that I would eventually be diagnosed with Breast Cancer? Or that I would be so blessed today. I know I do not face this diagnosis alone. I am blessed to be surrounded by amazing family and friends. Scott and I walked with the team again this year on Mother's Day and the cause certainly had new meaning. And so do the friendships we have developed over the last few years in our Hyatt family.

"Love cures people, both the ones who give it and the ones who receive it."   Dr. Karl Menninger

Postcard 41
What A Wonderful Week!

Sunday, May 16, 2010, 4:05 p.m.

This past week I enjoyed feeling better each day. Since the week began with head shaving, it wasn't exactly off to a stellar start, but as I contemplate the past 7 days, I have to say that they have been filled with treasured moments. Moments when I actually felt like my old self. Moments when I actually forgot I had cancer. I am learning to appreciate and savor these precious times more each day instead of taking them for granted. Since my last chemo was on a Friday and this second round tomorrow actually falls on a Monday, I feel I was treated to a "bonus weekend!" I tried to make the most of it and get out of the house. Here are just a handful of the things that made my week...

~ lunch with a friend

~ flowers, fragrances and funny cards from my kids

~ cooking a chicken and mashed potato dinner for the family

~ sweet comments from friends about my new "wig-ali-cious" hairdo

~ a handmade with love satin pillowcase

~ a ladies' night out

~ several hugs when I needed them

~ a bike ride on the Mission Beach Boardwalk

~ some fan gear I received to support my favorite football team, the Indianapolis Colts

~ a breakfast burrito at Taco Surf

99

~ a cheery note and drawings from some sweet little children
~ a pink "save the Ta-Ta's" cocktail
~ an Old Navy sale
~ holding a precious little baby
~ breakfast at Kono's beachside
~ singing some favorite hymns at church
~ top down on the TT wearing my wig with a hat to secure it (yikes!)
~ a precious handmade treasure made with love by precious young fingers

"Savor little glimpses of God's goodness and His majesty, thankful for the gift of them; winding pathways through the woods, a bright green canopy overhead, and dappled sunshine falling all around, warm upon our faces." from *Love is... Promise Journal*

A sweet Pink Warrior Sheep! Handmade with love
by my childhood friend's daughter Josie

Postcard 42
2 Down, 2 To Go!

Monday, May 17, 2010, 5:50 p.m.

I have a quick post tonight. Chemo Round 2 was uneventful. And we made it home before 7 p.m. Today I was a "guinea pig" for the Scripps Green Cancer Center's brand new chemo treatment room. It is beautiful and today was the opening day. Everything went without a glitch and the chairs were so comfortable. It made something not-so-nice, bearable. As far as side effects, this time I know what to expect and hopefully I can do more to prevent them. There is plenty to share from my oncologist appointment prior to the chemo. But tonight I am headed to bed as I didn't sleep much last night—a side effect from the Decadron I have to take the day before chemo, the day of and the day after. Insomnia isn't so bad when a marathon and the season finale of "Hollywood House Husbands" is running until 2 a.m. Scott doesn't share my passion for that show and he was blissfully "sawing logs" while I binge-watched. But tonight it's my turn to hit the pillow snoring. Tomorrow our local weatherman has called for a "2nd stage Drizzle Alert!" Not even kidding. Gotta love San Diego weather!

Postcard 43
Me—A Zebra? NOT a Turkey!

Wednesday May 19, 2010, 5:49 p.m.

Today is my second day out from Chemo Round 2. I am tired and starting to develop the dry mouth and sore throat again, but I am pretty sure my mind is in tact. So if this post sounds a little strange, trust me, I am seriously quoting my oncologist. On Monday at my doctor's appointment, I asked Dr. K some deeper questions regarding the Oncotype DX test results we received several weeks ago (see post from Thursday, April 15). This test came back with a very high recurrence score for my cancer and was in conflict with other pathology reports with regards to Estrogen Receptors on my cancer. These receptors are very important regarding treatments down the road, such as tamoxifen.

In revisiting the Oncotype DX result, my doctor confirmed again that she had not seen anything like it. She also reassured me that with the high-numbered result that chemotherapy treatment is the best thing I could possibly be doing to fight off this cancer and, of course, that is very encouraging. We also discussed and confirmed that I would follow the chemotherapy with radiation treatments. I will also take tamoxifen (a daily pill form hormone therapy) which will benefit me if I truly have positive estrogen receptors.

I was (and still am) feeling great about our decisions for treatment given my unique results. Then we broached the subject of the results of the BRCA Gene test that I had taken in April. This test is a simple blood test for me, but a complicated test for the lab. At the lab, the DNA is broken down into sequences (called genes) and certain genes are examined to determine if they contain mutations. BRCA-1 and BRCA-2 gene testing is used as a predictor for whether a gene I carry from my parents might put me (and other relatives who also have the gene) at greater risk for Breast Cancer. My oncologist looked at the result she said, "I guess you are just going to be my "zebra" in a herd of horses!" The results are peculiar once again. Though we didn't get into the results at length, because she wants to thoroughly review it before our next appointment, (sound familiar?), I will tell you what I do know. There are 2 genes that they test for: BRCA-1 and BRCA-2. Our genes are a long string of nucleotides. These advance tests look for mutations which can indicate that the individual is prone to a cancer diagnosis. Apparently, I *do* have a mutation in one of these genes (not sure which one yet) but it is a mutation on a nucleotide that scientists have *not* done considerable testing.

So I am "mutated?" What else is new? Probably no shock to the rest of my family! I have been labeled a "turkey" by my brother, Gene, since I was 10. He has provided plenty of reminders of my "turkey status" to me over the years. But now, a ZEBRA? That's news.

> *You alone created my inner being. You knitted me together inside my mother. I will give thanks to you because I have been so amazingly and miraculously made. Your works are miraculous and my soul is fully aware of this.*
> Psalm 139:13-14 GOD'S WORD Translation

Postcard 44
Rockin' that Wig

Friday, May 21, 2010, 2:51 p.m.

Happy Friday!

It's gonna be gorgeous here in San Diego and I am planning on getting out a little to enjoy it. I also want you to know that I believe I have come "full circle" on this hair loss thing. Today, I actually laughed out loud when I realized I was looking forward to slapping on my wig and getting out of this apartment for a bit. I have been stuck between the couch and the bed ever since chemo Monday. Some fresh air sounds good. And so does a different look in the mirror!

In an effort to be comfortable, I don't wear a wig around the house. But it feels weird if my bald head is uncovered (and it's cold!) so I wear comfy little scarfs or caps. Every time I see my reflection in the mirror as I wander around the apartment, I am either scarf-laden or night-capped. Ugh. Somehow, right now, that wig sounds great! What a change of heart in a few days time. I conquered Chemo Round 2 this past Monday as you can see in the photo. My daughter saw the photo and said I was "rockin' that wig!" I don't get that response from her with my real hair!?! So it seems that half of this chemo business is behind me. And that is fabulous! Time to get out and "rock" the weekend!

Chemo Round 2

Postcard 45
Hair Today, Gone Tomorrow

Friday, May 28, 2010, 7:01 p.m.

Even though my scalp is shaved, the short little hairs that remained from the number 2 clipper are now succumbing to the chemo drugs and falling out, in handfuls. When I got out of the shower with a multitude of tiny hairs covering my towel, fragments of a verse came to me from when I was a little girl in Lutheran grade school—something about God knowing how many hairs were on my head.

As a child, I remember marveling at this thought. I have always had a lot of hair. Over the last few weeks, I am certain God has had to frequently check my "status" to get an accurate count. I lose so many short little hairs off my buzzed head during the day when I am wearing my little cap, yet I still have some hair on my head. Not a lot, but some. Scott noted the other night that I am well on my way to a "mohawk" since the sides and back of my hair have come off first. Maybe because they rub against my pillow. My balding is just one of the many ugly sides of this disease. I belong to several discussion boards on breastcancer.org and every day I read stories of many women who face much more than hair loss in their battles with breast cancer.

Of course many women face the loss of their breasts or their beautiful figure, either with weight loss or gain, and some lose their ability to be active. Others' losses are even more substantial, like a husband in divorce, or friends who abandon because they don't know how to help. I am blessed.

I have a supportive and loving husband and family, and amazing friends who are right there for me, at my ugliest. But above that I know that my God is with me too. I looked up that verse that I remembered from grade school. It is Luke 12:6-7 and it says: *"Are not five sparrows sold for two cents? Yet not one of them is forgotten before God. Indeed, the very hairs of your head are all numbered. Do not fear; you are more valuable than many sparrows."* I can't imagine facing this disease without the comfort of my faith, yet many women do. This Pink Warrior is empowered by the thought that I am valuable to God, not insignificant, not forgotten by God. He sees my mohawk and loves me just the same. I hope the comfort in this verse encourages you, like it does me. I know that I am not the only one facing trials or possibly feeling "forgotten." Know that you are significant, you are loved.

Postcard 46
It's Memorial Day!

Monday, May 31, 2010, 4:14 p.m.

So today is Memorial Day and I couldn't be happier. It seems like so much has happened since my diagnosis on February 22nd. That's 3 months ago. I am happy because time is passing and I am making progress in my treatments. I am half way through chemo and on my way to a well deserved break between chemo and radiation treatments. On the 4th of July I should be done with chemo, and by Labor Day weekend nearly finished with radiation.

Today, Memorial Day, we honor those who died in war. My heart goes out to the scores of families who lost their loved one while he or she was serving our country. I am forever grateful for those who fought and died with courage. When I was growing up, I remember each year on Memorial Day weekend my mom and my Aunt Gladys would get a flat of petunias and some geraniums at the local nursery and head to the cemetery. We were there to honor our family members who had passed away. None of them died in war, but many had served in the military in war time, and they were all worth remembering. We planted flowers at the tombstones of my grandparents (who I had never met) and at their little daughter Ruth's, grave. She died at a very young age from scarlet fever. As the years went on, we planted flowers at my Uncle Wilmer's grave and at my dad's.

I remember my mom would bring a coffee can and fill it with water and fresh cuts of orange blossoms from our home to place on my father's headstone. She said my dad used to love them. I moved away from that Indiana farm at age 18, 2 years after my mom died, but once or twice when I went back to Indiana for Memorial Day weekend I left flowers at her grave. And I took my children. It's important to remember and to honor those who lived before, those who made us who we are, and those who fought to make our country great. Of course, Memorial Day weekend wouldn't have been complete years ago without a good barbecue and a game of croquet or "jarts" (large lawn darts that we would try to throw into circle targets on the lawn—a rather dangerous game as I think of it now, but when I was young, kids were allowed more reckless play I think—and we all survived). Some 30 years later the celebrations continue with grilled meat and spicy sauce and a safer game of "corn hole." And even though I can't visit that cemetery in Indiana, I can still honor them. It's Memorial Day — relax and remember.

Postcard 47
Itchy and Scratchy

Tuesday, June 1, 2010, 6:50 p.m.

Are you familiar with "The Itchy and Scratchy Show?" It is a show within a show, a cartoon that is part of The Simpsons series. Well, today I am. "Itchy and Scratchy" that is. And it's a show within a show, an allergic reaction in addition to the chemo side effects I have been experiencing. D'oh! Not sure where I picked up this lovely experience, but if you could see me today you would agree that I could be the star! I could also qualify for the role of "Krusty, the Clown." Itchy, Scratchy, Krusty... sign me up! I'm not sure what exactly caused this lovely reaction. Maybe I was bitten by some weird insect on a ride in the convertible. Or, even though I have enjoyed them all my life, it could be the shrimp I shelled and ate that didn't agree with me. Something triggered this reaction that has been building over the last 36 hours. Today I can report hives the size of golf balls on all of my extremities and the itch to go along with it. I visited an allergy specialist today who couldn't pinpoint a cause, but I don't really care as long as the medications he prescribed bring me back to my "normal" zebra self! It's not so bad, I guess in the cartoon world I'd rather be Itchy or Scratchy than the Grinch!

Be cheerful no matter what.
1 Thessalonians 5:18 The Message

Postcard 48
Happy Hour Monday!

Sunday June 6, 2010, 9:46 p.m.

Tomorrow at 2 p.m. is "Happy Hour." Time for Round 3 chemo "cocktail." After that I will have only one more treatment remaining. Over the past 21 days, I have had few "good" days but my husband and I have tried to make them not just good, but amazing! Our wedding anniversary last week was a good day. That day I felt good enough to cook dinner and we enjoyed a lovely "Table for 2" at our haven on the roof. And then, after my bout with "Itchy and Scratchy" and my "quarantine" time of low blood counts was over, Scott thought we should enjoy a little getaway.

Friday after work he came home and said "pack a bag!" He had made reservations in Las Vegas! As a chemo patient, I know I wasn't the typical Vegas visitor, but I am pretty sure that I wasn't the only one there "rockin'" a wig! Though I was a bit apprehensive that I might not be up for it, we truly had a nice, relaxing time away. The highlight for me was Barry Manilow's show. It was one of those shows were you can sing-a-long with every song and we both did. It's amazing what a little "Can't Smile Without You" can do for your soul. Even my "evil pseudo persona" that I have developed on this latest dose of steroids (see the next postcard) couldn't resist singing and smiling with the one who "Writes the Songs!" I plan to add a few Manilow classics to that "Happy Hour" playlist.

Postcard 49
Not A Texas Longhorn Fan, But...

Wednesday, June 9, 2010, 5:37 p.m.

Scott and I are not University of Texas Longhorn fans but we've seen a lot of their famous "horns" hand signal lately! In my previous post, I eluded to my "pseudo evil persona" and it has been making a few appearances. When I went in for the "itchy and scratchys" last week, the allergy doc prescribed a round of steroids. Along with all of my chemo treatments, I have been taking steroids for 3 days before and after and haven't noticed any big changes in my personality. But this latest weeklong packet of pills is a whole new ball game.

Within a day or two, I came out of my shell and "locked horns" with Scott and a few others as well. Yikes. It seemed appropriate to us that this new behavior should be symbolized by the Longhorn fan hand symbol. (Think index finger and pinky extended, like horns.) Scott and I have adopted this "signal" to mean, "Jan, you are pushing it and locking horns! So stop whatever you are doing!" This secret signal may have saved me a black eye when I nearly kicked and pushed the man out of the way who simply cut in front of me in line in Vegas! Who knows how that might have ended up?

Sad to say, my loving husband is definitely taking the brunt of my new "evil persona." We sat down at Pink's (World Famous Hot Dogs) on the Strip in Vegas. He offered me half of his sweet relish covered dog and, of course, he should know (he is my husband after all!) that I don't like sweet relish. But he insisted and started cutting the dog in two. In my scariest "exorcist" voice, I proceeded to tell him, "Don't give me that! I don't like sweet relish!" (watch out for my plastic fork headed your way...) Wow...

Thankfully, I finished the steroid pack and am back to couch potato after chemo round 3! Only one more to go in a couple weeks. And even better, Scott's still alive to talk about it.

> *Create in me a clean heart, O God; and RENEW A RIGHT SPIRIT WITHIN ME.* (emphasis mine)
> Psalm 51:10 KJV

Postcard 50
A Boo-Yah For Bette

Friday, June 11, 2010, 6:35 p.m.

Who hasn't heard the song, "Wind Beneath My Wings?" Some of you may love this Bette Midler classic and yet many others may cringe, thinking it's overplayed or overhyped. This week while I have been contemplating my lowly state, the song has been running through my mind.

On Monday, before I went to my chemotherapy session, I saw my oncologist for a quick checkup, as usual. While there, Dr. K commented that I have been doing, "Great! Really great!" with these treatments. "Way better than average" she said. Hmm? "Way better than average." I have had plenty of couch time this week to contemplate why. I read blogs and discussion boards daily bursting with posts from women who are suffering through terrible physical and emotional side effects.

This is not an simple disease, where you simply "take a pill" and the symptoms go away. I wish it was. It sure would be a lot easier. In my humble experience what is making this chemotherapy "do-able" is the incredible support I have received from family and friends. I want to be clear that I trust in my God and that I know He makes "All things (even chemo!) work together for good for those that love Him" and I rest every day on that promise. But I have to say that since I started this journey the love and support from others is, as Bette croons, "the wind beneath my wings."

Here are just a few of the things that get me through each day: working word puzzle books, reading emails, glancing down at the bracelet I am wearing for a reminder that someone cares, savoring the sweetness of my own ice cream flavor "Jan's Tranquilo Moments" (eCreamery.com), browsing through sweet cards and letters, relaxing in comfy pajamas with soft slipper socks on my feet, reading borrowed books, jotting notes to friends on beautiful handmade note cards, sipping smoothies, gazing at flowers delivered (saved forever on that jpg file on my hard drive), reading timely text messages and listening to caring voicemails, munching yummy homemade cookies, enjoying the indulgence of a soft lotion, browsing through a magazine. As I think of all those pleasures, it sounds more like I am on vacation than in chemotherapy, right? So you see my point—kind and thoughtful gifts and messages carry me through this time and truly are the "wind beneath my wings!"

*"The eagle that soars at great altitudes does not worry about how it will cross a river."*Unknown

Postcard 51
Twitchy, Itchy, Witchy Chickie

Monday, June 21, 2010, 7:48 p.m.

I have issues right now. Or I guess I should say my body has issues. Trust me, I have always had some issues! My close friends will tell you that. But I am talking about some strange stuff going on now due to the chemo medicine. I have been quiet with no posts for about 10 days and the reason is that as the treatments go on the fatigue has been deeper. (And as my mama said, "Nothing good to say? Don't say anything!")

But today I thought I would share some of the stranger side effects I have been experiencing. The "pink plagues" continue, but in addition I have developed some weird stuff. For one thing, my eyes are not only tearing up a lot more, but they are twitchy. Both of them. Oftentimes during the day my eyelids or my lower lashes with start random movement. Annoying, but at least it is barely visible to others. Also, I am getting a lot of itching this time and, though my rash is milder, I get hives wherever I scratch. Of course, I am trying my best to lay off the scratching. Also, one of the side effects possible with Taxotere is that your fingernails and toenails can turn black and fall off. I have been faithfully putting tea tree oil on my cuticles to help prevent this and so far so good. But, I do have some gray under my nail and my fingernails have a few ridges in them now. They look a bit witchy. And my hair is almost completely gone (though Scott says I still have more than he does! and he's right.) The hair I do have left following the buzz cut and it falling out is about an inch long and very

117

soft. I think I look like a baby bird with a little fuzz on the top, like the little chicks we used to raise on the farm when I was little.

I have come to realize that there actually are a few good things about losing hair, like not having to shave my legs for weeks. But today I looked at the incision near my right armpit (from my lymph node removal) to make sure it was healing well and I saw 2 long black "lines." I thought, "What in the world?!?" Much to my chagrin, they were actually 2 long armpit hairs! I couldn't believe it! I can't grow a hair on my head, but my armpit looks like its on Rogaine! This twitchy, itchy, witchy chickie has issues. But I am happy to report that my fourth and FINAL chemo is scheduled for the afternoon of Wednesday, June 30.

> *God cares for you, so turn all your worries over*
> *to Him.* 1 Peter 5:7 CEV

Postcard 52
The Soothing Sun

Saturday, June 26, 2010, 7:16 a.m.

The past few days have been wonderful! This was supposed to be my "good" week between chemo treatments and with the rough start I had on Monday, Scott decided to get us out of wicked routine and rent a condo at the beach. It's difficult to express how healing the ocean breeze is and how soothing the sun. I have enjoyed every minute! Some time on the seashore makes such a difference. I have enjoyed relaxing on a lounge chair in the sand, playing a little game of "pickle" with my sweet Savannah in the ocean surf, kicking back on a boat cruise watching dolphins play, and have all but forgotten I have cancer. Back to my reality soon, but for now I'll take it.

26/06/2010

Beach days with Savannah

Postcard 53
'Twas The Night Before My Last Chemo

Tuesday, June 29, 2010, 9:13 p.m.

Twas the night before my LAST chemo, when all through
our hotel
All the staff was working, including as always, my
friend Adele.
My hospital bag was packed with care,
In hopes that adequate entertainment would be f
ound in there.
Zack and Savannah were nestled all snug in their beds,
While visions of the County Fair danced in their heads.
And Scott in his "nurse's scrubs," and I in my
"bald chick" cap,
Had just settled our brains for a long restful nap.
When out on the roof there arose such a clatter,
I sprang from the bed to see what was the matter.
Away to the window I flew like a flash,
Tore open the shutters and threw up the sash.
The moon on the breast of the San Diego "marine layer"
Gave the luster of mid-day to my personal haven up there.
When, what shocked my wondering eyes out of sleep,
But a flock of turkeys, a herd of zebras and
several random sheep.
With a beautiful angel, so glowing and bright,
I knew in a moment it was going to be alright.
On the wings of eagles, His messenger came
And she sang, and shouted, and called me by name!

"Pink Warrior! Pink Warrior! Now, Pink Warrior, LISTEN!
Be confident! There is nothing that you are missing!
Tomorrow you'll enter that chemotherapy stall,
For the medicine that will clear away,
clear away, clear away all!"
As dry leaves that before the wild hurricane fly,
When they meet with an obstacle, mount to the sky.
So up to the house-top, my worries they flew,
With the beautiful angel, and the presence of God too.
And then, in a twinkling I knew on the roof
That in the angels words I had my proof.
As I drew in my head, and was turning around,
The joy in my heart knew no bound.
Though bald and achy from my head to my feet,
Even so I knew now this Pink Warrior was complete.
That burden of fear I had carried on my back,
Had just disappeared. My future was bright and not black.
My eyes, how they twitched! My "zebra stripes," how merry!
My scars were like roses, my bald head, not so scary!
My grumbling little mouth was drawn up like a bow,
No complaints now, but ready to share the hope that I know.
The sword of the Spirit the angel held tight in her sheath,
And glory encircled her head like a wreath.
The zebras, turkeys and sheep were a bit smelly,
But they made me chuckle, like a bowlful of jelly!
I am chubby and plump, a right jolly old elf,
And I laughed when I saw them, in spite of myself!
A wink from the angel's eye and a twist of her head,
Soon gave me to know I had nothing to dread.
She spoke these words straight from heaven to her work,

"The Lord our God's with you, He is mighty to save, He will take great delight in you and rejoice over you!" (Zephaniah 3:17)

then she drew up her wings and turned with a jerk.
Knowing she had answered all my woes,
And giving a nod, back up to heaven she rose!
She sprang to the sky, to the animals gave a whistle,
And away they all flew like the down of a thistle.
But I heard her exclaim, 'ere she disappeared out of sight,
"Happy Hour tomorrow to all, and to all a good-night!"

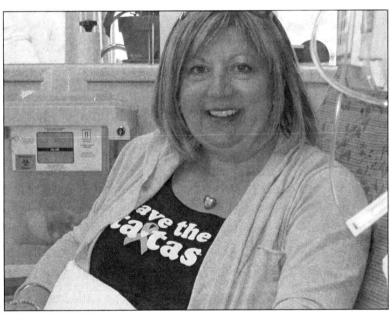

Final Chemotherapy Treatment, June 30

Postcard 54
Disturbing The Peace

Sunday, July 4, 2010, 8:38 p.m.

Do your thoughts ever betray you? This is the situation I have been in when trying to sleep the last few nights. Generally the 2nd and 3rd night after a treatment (which I had on Wednesday) are tough sleeping. My oncologist gives me a little "nighty night" pill to help, but still I wake up at some point (usually to visit the restroom, since I am drinking more than a liter of water every hour during the day to minimize side effects). And then when I wake up, my brain is full of weird and twisted things. Things that have some foundation in reality, but become overblown or confused in the middle of the night when mixed with medicated state. Last night my thoughts continually drifted to "criminal" me.

For starters, I must confess to a lead foot in the car. It runs in my family. My sister can tell more than a few of her own stories. But over the last year since my son Zack, has been driving, Savannah has become the in-car audible speedometer. If she's in the car, no worries, you will know if you are speeding! Who needs a Tom-Tom to signal the indiscretion? She will announce without hesitation if you are driving 5 or 25 miles over the speed limit. Though Zack and I both cringe when she tells us "Slow Down!," I know we are both secretly grateful. Last week I was out driving and unfortunately Savannah had slept in and stayed home. And, of course, as I go 64mph in a 45 there's an unmarked police officer right there on the berm. Lights start flashing, I pull over and just a few minutes later I was leaving with the prize... a big, fat ticket! And the event became even more unbelievable when I got home and looked the fine up on the internet. Are you kidding me? I need to start selling all my worldly possessions to pay this one off. And this is what was keeping me up last night.

All night I tossed and turned, only to wake up with "flashing lights" in my dreams. How miserable. Now I know that the medicines I have been taking are truly responsible for this nighttime criminal mind of mine, but today I began thinking how my thoughts can disturb my "peace" on daily basis. My niece recently sent me a magnet which says, "Peace. It does not mean to be in a place where there is no noise, trouble, or hard work. It means to be in the midst of those things and still be calm in your heart." (Anonymous) Tonight when I lay my head on my pillow I will pray for peaceful dreams and a good night's sleep, but through this breast cancer journey, I know that I do have true peace, the peace expressed on the magnet, peace that passes understanding.

> *I give you peace, the kind of peace that only I can give. It isn't like the peace that this world can give. So don't be worried or afraid.* (This was a reading at our wedding in 2005)
> John 14:27 Contemporary English Version

Postcard 55
Turning A Corner

Saturday, July 10, 2010, 7:13 p.m.

After completing all my chemotherapy treatments about two weeks ago, I have been very tired. It seems the treatments have a cumulative effect. Today I cannot even begin to share with you how elated I am to move forward. I have an appointment with my medical oncologist, Dr. K, in mid-July to discuss our future strategies and make necessary life-preserving decisions. On the 21st of this month, I have a consult with the radiation oncologist to plan my radiation treatments. I have been told that I will have 35 treatments, once a day (Monday-Friday) for 7 weeks. Some say these are much easier than the chemo with fatigue and skin soreness, similar to a sunburn, being the worst of the side effects. Right now I feel as if I am "turning a corner" and heading down a different stretch of road. I have chemo in the rearview mirror and radiation ahead, not quite coasting downhill yet but getting closer. It is kind thoughts from caring friends that shine light on the road of this stretch of my journey.

> *"Impart as much as you can of your spiritual being to those who are on the road with you, and accept as something precious what comes back to you from them."*   Albert Schweitzer

Postcard 56
Stop And Smell The Daisies

Tuesday, July 13, 2010, 9:55 p.m.

Do daisies even smell? I don't think so. But they surely are beautiful. My kids, Zack and Savannah are spending the summer with me. They have been so understanding, helpful and encouraging as I recuperate from the last chemo. I have a bit more energy now and we are able to get out and enjoy our gorgeous city and each other. This past week we visited one of the museums in San Diego's stunning Balboa Park. As we passed by the flower garden, the daisies were so lovely we couldn't help but stop. I took a few photos of them and then a gentleman sitting nearby enjoying his lunch offered to take a photo of us. Wherever you are, guy-eating-lunch, I am grateful. It was so nice of him because the subjects and setting of this photo are special.

My time with my kids is so precious and the garden was spectacular. Isn't it nice how a photo can take you back in time? Gazing at this photo, I can almost hear the bees buzzing the blooms. The picture holds the moment in time and will forever be a reminder to me. A reminder to take time out. How many times have you heard the advice, "stop and smell the roses?" but how often do you really do it? Traveling along this new road, I am learning a lot about myself and about what truly matters in life. I believe one of the most important things is to "stop" each day and take notice of my many blessings, to be thankful for the many gifts I have been given, and to inhale the intoxicating scent of life.

At Balboa Park, San Diego with Zack and Savannah

Postcard 57
From Wigs and Weight Gain to Hormones and Hot Flashes

Monday, July 19, 2010, 9:47 p.m.

I am entering a new phase on this journey. Today my oncologist and her staff gave me praise and congratulations on completing the chemo treatments and that felt great. They were full of encouragement—the worst was over, my hair will be coming back (apparently it starts growing back 8 weeks after the final treatment—that's 5 weeks from now), my energy will be increasing (she recommended starting an exercise regimen to jumpstart that), and the allergic reactions, rashes, hives will be subsiding. No more steroids—which means, hopefully, no more weight gain. I am moving on!

Next up on my "itinerary" is hormone treatment. I received a prescription today for tamoxifen. We are going forward with this hormone treatment to "starve" the cancer cells, though my doctor is not completely confident that the tumor was estrogen receptor positive. You may remember from previous posts that several tests came back with conflicting results. However, the treatment works so well on ER+ cancers that we are going to go ahead and use this strategy, believing that I am at least marginally ER+. The tamoxifen will bring with it early menopause and of course the added bonus of hot flashes.

Get ready, I am becoming "one hot mamma!" I will be seeing the radiation oncologist next week, but I am released from medical oncology for 3 months. I am happy to be married to a good sport, because as we left the medical onc's office today she reminded us that by the time I see her again I should have more hair than Scott does!

> *My brothers and sisters, be very happy when you are tested in different ways. You know that such testing of your faith produces endurance.*
> James 1:2-3 GOD'S WORD Translation

Postcard 58
Tickled Pink

Wednesday, July 28, 2010, 10:20 p.m.

My husband and I have been married just over 5 years now. I know when we married he did not sign up for this cancer thing, but without a doubt, he has been more wonderful than I could ever have imagined. The last few months have been no fun. I mean really. Through these posts you have an idea of what I have been going through, but it is a whole different matter living with me.

Every day, sometimes every hour, I have a different ache or pain or symptom or mood! I am fearful, then I am confident. I am comfortable, then I am sore. I am awake, then I am suddenly asleep. I am hungry and then the thought of food makes me gag. I am overweight and I want to shop to buy new clothes, then I am disgusted with my weight and am determined to diet and fit into all the cute clothes in my closet. I am bald, then I am sporting an unfamiliar wig (and Scott can't find me in a store—sad, but true, story). I am laughing. I am crying. I am, in a word, unpredictable. But through it all, he has been amazingly predictable. And his love for me unfailing.

A few years ago the two of us discovered a book called the "Five Love Languages" by Gary Chapman. It is an enlightening book that talks about how everyone has a different love "language" and that even though you love someone, if you don't "speak" to them in their love language then they don't truly receive your love. The five love languages are Words of Affirmation, Quality Time, Receiving Gifts, Acts of Service, and Physical Touch.

For example, let's say your spouse's love "language" is Words of Affirmation; however, you try to show him/her that you love them by cooking dinner and mowing the lawn (Acts of Service) but never tell them they are a terrific mother/father/spouse, then they will have a hard time feeling loved. Think about yourself. What says "I love you" to you? Is it when your spouse does the laundry (Acts of Service) that you know he/she loves you or is it when he/she sits down on the couch with you after a long hard day of work (Quality Time)?

For me, I appreciate help around the house and I enjoy spending time with Scott, but I feel love through receiving gifts. It has been this way as long as I can remember. Maybe it was because when I was a little girl on the farm we didn't have a lot of money and I knew when my parents bought me something, they used precious funds and it meant they loved me. It doesn't have to be a big gift, in fact sometimes the smallest or least expensive gifts are the most treasured. Don't mistake this love language for materialism; the receiver of gifts thrives on the love, thoughtfulness, and effort behind the gift. I am a fortunate wife because Scott has some serious skills as a "gift-giver." One of his assistants at work was surprised to learn that when Christmas or my birthday rolls around he just takes a notecard from a secret space in his desk and heads to the mall.

Throughout the year, he has jotted down things on this notecard that I have mentioned that I could use or would like to have. The notecard is his shopping list, ready to go! The question is, what do you get a girl who just finished chemo?

In his heart, I know he felt that something should mark this milestone in my treatment. Just after my last chemo, Scott decided to attend a local auction and he found the perfect gift, the perfect thing to make a bald girl feel beautiful, the perfect thing to mark this milestone for his Pink Warrior, a beautiful pink sapphire and diamond bracelet. I will wear it always to remind me that through God's grace and mercy and the love of family and friends I survived chemo. The phrase "tickled pink" means "filled with sublime emotion." Even though I may be unpredictable, right now I am Tickled Pink!

"Real love is always a gift from God; a gift of Himself."　　　　　　　　　　Eugenia Price

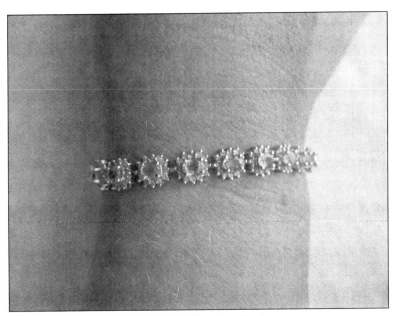

Pink Rocks from my Rock

Postcard 59
"Scripps Ink" Tatts Up Pink Warrior!

Friday, July 30, 2010, 9:21 a.m.

This morning I woke up with 3 tattoos! And no, I wasn't dreaming! I didn't have any tattoos before and never wanted any, but was shocked to find out this is actually part of the radiation treatments. They are very tiny and look just like a dot made with a Sharpie marker. Yesterday at the Scripps radiation oncology center I had my radiation consultation, simulation and subsequent tattoo session. First I met briefly with a nurse who discussed with me the side effects of radiation treatments. I will be having 35 treatments, Monday through Friday daily beginning next week for 7 weeks. She said I should expect fatigue (Not much of a surprise. It seems to me that just going to the Dr's office every day for 7 weeks will make me tired!) and also burns and discomfort to my breast. Not a big shock either.

The nurse mentioned that I should get some Aloe Gel. Had I ever heard of it? Funny. I used to live in Aruba and Aloe just happens to be Aruba's number one export, so yes, I am very familiar! During the 7 week time period, aloe is the only thing I am allowed to apply to my right side. No cologne, no deodorant, no exfoliating body washes in the shower, and no shaving. Great. This could get stinky.

After the nurse consult, she took me into the CT scan room where I laid on the scan board while they spent over an hour "decorating" me with stickers and markers and then took lots of photos. The stickers and marks help them line up the lasers for the treatment. They took a CT scan and did several adjustments until they got it right. Then the technician pulled out the india ink and needles and put two tiny tattoos on my breastbone and one under my arm. Now I have permanent indicators to insure accurate radiation treatment.

Next Thursday I will have my first session. A "Happy Hour" again as I maneuver into another battle phase that will bring this Pink Warrior closer to the end, to the cancer's surrender. At that appointment I will receive my "Rad Plan" which will give me exact dates and times for my treatments. Leaving the office, I was a bit stunned about the tattoo session, but I was even more in shock, when, as we got in the car my son said, "Mom, now you can't say anything about me getting a tattoo because you have three!" (not funny!)

Postcard 60
An Old Scar

Saturday, August 7, 2010, 1:14 p.m.

I have been in a fragile state the last couple of days. I am sure that is has had something to do with my children heading back to Ohio after a fun summer. And something to do with starting a new treatment to fight the cancer. Perhaps something to do with trying to get back into a routine as chemo and its nasty side effects become a thing of the past. I also think it has to do with the hormones (or lack of hormones) raging in my body. The tamoxifen is interfering with my estrogen now and I am sure that has heightened my emotions and is rendering me close to tears on a moment's notice. Any number of things can have me in need of a kleenex.

Not the least of which is my lack of hair. I know that you probably are sick of hearing about it. To some extent as it was falling out I just "got over it"; but now that chemo is 6 weeks behind me I am on constant "Hair Watch," I have doubts. Doubts if my hair will return and what it will be like. I know it may sound strange, but it's true. I am checking on an hour by hour basis to see if I have stubble on my legs or hair growing anywhere else. I have read true "nightmares" of women who had minimal hair growth on their scalp for months following chemo, but needed to shave their upper lip every other day. Oy! I am praying every day that won't be me.

So far, so good. This past week I actually had Scott shave my scalp to get rid of the very few inch-long hairs I had retained through treatment so that the "new" hair would come in even and easily trackable! Am I obsessed or what? I also realize that the new hair is probably going to be very different from my old hair. Today Scott said he saw a few hairs coming in and they were brown. Brown? But I am a natural blonde. I am scared. Better brown than gray though, right? As I went to the bathroom mirror to check, I had to get out the hand mirror to see the back, not something I have wanted to do in the last few months! What I saw stopped me in my tracks.

I had a scar on the back of my head in the center of my scalp. I had never seen that before. It had always been covered with hair. But seeing that scar helped me remember. I remembered my mom and dad telling the story of the accident that happened when I was 4 years old. I fell off the back porch on the farm and cut my head open on a foot scraper. A story I had long forgotten, but now at 45 years old, thousands of miles away from my childhood home of New Haven, Indiana, my bald head showed visible evidence.

It got me thinking. The doubts I have aren't all about my hair. They are doubts about myself too. Part of my fragile state has to do with wondering if I am going to be the same—the same wife, mother, friend, sister that I was before I heard the dreaded words, "You have cancer." Strangely, the scar was comforting.

I am the same person. The scar is proof of my history. Proof of where I come from and a part of who I have become. That scar from a little fall at age 4 is a good symbol of all my life experiences. All the things I have been through in my life, big and small, including the cancer, have made me who I am today, Saturday, August 7, 2010. I am not the only one who has been comforted by a scar. After Jesus died on the cross, he appeared to a few of his disciples. Men who I am sure were also filled with doubt about their future. But seeing Jesus' scars from the cross on his hands and feet reassured them that He was who He said He was all along. All the rules had now changed, Jesus hung on a cross and died and then rose and was alive to share his "scars." And life would go on, but even better than before. That same reassurance is mine today that I am still me, even though some of the things that have defined me in the past, like my hair, have changed. I am becoming who God created me to be and my life will go on, maybe even better than before.

Postcard 61
4th Down, 32 To Go

Tuesday, August 10, 2010 11:50 a.m.

And I am not talking about football...though I am excited that football season is here. It's amazing to me that it is that time again. You know the Super Bowl was played on February 7 of this year and I was diagnosed on February 22. I should have known then it was going to be a rough year since my Indianapolis Colts lost the big game.

Looking back, I have spent much of the time between now and then in a major fog. So it came as a pleasant surprise when the Bengals-Cowboys preseason game was on TV the other night. Wow! Football's back! And I am really looking forward to enjoying the season. Right now I have 4 radiation treatments behind me! And compared to chemo, they are a breeze! Though the treatment is fairly simple so far, I can truly say that I never imagined I would be rolling out of bed, getting dressed, driving to a clinic, getting undressed, laying on a board bare-breasted, getting measured, adjusted and x-rayed, redressing and driving home by 8am each morning! Really? But alas, that is my routine Monday through Friday for the next 6 weeks.

But the weekends are for FOOTBALL! My dear Colts will have played 4 preseason and 2 regular season games by the time I finish radiation treatments. I will be looking forward to each weekend so I can relax and watch the games. The side effects from radiation have been minimal so far. I have been faithful applying the aloe, or should I say Scott has! (I must admit I think he is enjoying his nursing duties for once.) And even though we are football fans, not baseball, we are certainly doing our part to save 2nd base!

> *"Every time you are able to find some humor in a difficult situation, you win."*　　Unknown

Postcard 62
Attitude Is Everything!

Thursday, August 12, 2010, 9:20 a.m.

A friend of mine sent me this today and I had to share:

There once was a woman who woke up one morning, looked in the mirror, and noticed she had only three hairs on her head.

Well," she said, "I think I'll braid my hair today." So she did and she had a wonderful day.

The next day she woke up, looked in the mirror and saw that she had only two hairs on her head.

"H-M-M," she said, "I think I'll part my hair down the middle today." So she did and she had a grand day.

The next day she woke up, looked in the mirror and noticed that she had only one hair on her head.

"Well," she said, "today I'm going to wear my hair in a pony tail." So she did and she had a fun, fun day.

The next day she woke up, looked in the mirror and noticed that there wasn't a single hair on her head.

"YEA!" she exclaimed, "I don't have to fix my hair today!" (author unknown)

I have learned to be content whatever the circumstances... Philippians 4:11b

Postcard 63
It's Five O'clock Somewhere...

Wednesday, August 18, 2010, 8:32 p.m.

And that "somewhere" is on my head! Pink Warrior "HairWatch Live" is reporting a "five o'clock shadow" on my scalp! Woo Hoo! I guess there is hope. Hope that one day I will be able to leave the wig at home. Hair grows VERY slow. I have been waiting and watching for a few weeks and finally I have news to report. My eyebrows also got very thin during the chemo, but I am thankful that I didn't lose all my eyebrows or eyelashes as many women do. Today I am happy to say I saw a few stragglers up there in what's left of my brow line. Right now it looks more like an untended garden than a well-groomed eyebrow but, hey, who's complaining? Not me. Just a few new hairs poking out from anywhere is encouraging.

I know that I will need patience, but anything good takes time, right? Like, for example, radiation treatments. Today I completed radiation treatment number 8 out of 36. I have begun to view it as my daily dip in the fryer. On the KFC (Kentucky Fried Chicken) scale of skin crispness, mine would qualify as "regular," and it still has a way to go to reach "extra crispy" status. The aloe regimen is working to keep me nice and cool. On another front, I am still having bouts with allergic reactions, skin itchiness and hives but its much milder than before. Slowly but surely, the storm is passing through.

"The joyful birds prolong the strain, their song with every spring renewed; the air we breathe, the falling rain, each softly whispers: God is good."   John Hampden Gurney

Postcard 64
Mystery Of The Missing Lashes

Tuesday, August 24, 2010, 5:04 p.m.

Enough already.

I am more than 7 weeks past my final chemo session and *now* my eyelashes decide to fall out. Ugh. Yesterday when I woke up I noticed that on my left eye I had a couple "bare" spots in my upper lash line. By last night all but about 2 little lashes were gone from below and this morning my right eyelashes are sparse. Not what I was expecting, now that I am starting to feel better and have a little energy. It may not seem like a big deal, but it is really annoying. I am not sure why those little rascals held out this long, but they did and I was excited about it. Now, I am bummed. It's a mystery, but they are gone like the wind. It's crazy how such a tiny thing, like an eyelash, in the scheme of life can seem so important.

That's one of the things that amazes me about this disease. It affects so many areas of life, big and small. If I am not careful these days, my emotions can be carried away on the wind as well. It is the compassion of friends that has really helped me to be strong and not succumb to the tidal wave of emotions. Maybe the lashes are gone so I can truly "see" around me. As I "look," I am truly amazed at the kindness sent my way, sometimes from the unlikeliest of places—my favorite flowers, sent from Germany; an unexpected basket full of very thoughtful treasures, delivered by precious members of my Hyatt family; a book, handmade by sweet first graders that illustrates my life "From Turkeys to Zebras"; an email from a travel agent who's been reading my posts and offers words of encouragement.

I believe this is how God shows his love to me, even in the toughest of times, through the love of others. I only hope that I can show the same love in return. The lashes will grow back (hopefully) and when they do I commit to use that moment each morning when I apply my mascara as a reminder. A reminder to keep my eyes open, to look for the needs of those around me and to show them real love.

> *Dear friends, let us love one another, for love comes from God. Everyone who loves has been born of God and knows God.* 1 John 4:7

Postcard 65
It's A Marathon...

Wednesday, September 1, 2010, 8:51 p.m.

...and I have never been much of a runner. But then I found this verse—I am re-energized, refreshed, restored, renewed reading Isaiah 46:4: "*Even to your old age and gray hairs I am he, I am he who will sustain you. I have made you and I will carry you; I will sustain you and I will rescue you.*" It's like a Red Bull and a Mood Enhancer all in one! And boy, do I need it! This week has been a tough one.

Yesterday I went into my early morning radiation treatment full of joy, practically bouncing onto the table declaring that, "Today is 'Hump Day' and after today's treatment, I will be *halfway* done!" But I knew something was wrong when the tech was getting me into position for treatment number 18 and she said, "Well, almost." Huh? After she finished her daily "zapping" she came back in and said, "Has the Dr. talked with you about the 'boost' treatments?"

WHAT?!? No, she hadn't. Come to find out, I have another simulation appointment next week to prepare me for radiation "boosts" which will be more targeted radiation to the tumor bed site. These treatments will follow the conclusion of my current 36 treatments. Hey! Now they're moving the finish line on me! Not cool. With the state of my hormones these days, the tech was lucky I didn't have a babbling, bawling meltdown right there in the radiation chamber. I managed to make it to the car before I completely lost it. I also managed to complain to a few dear friends before I got a comment that set me straight.

My friend Tracy put it plain and simple: "So what's a few more treatments? The doctors are being thorough and the Lord is your strength." She is so right. And you know what else? That's all *good, very* good.

And in other good news — on "Hair Watch 2010," I can report sprouting a full 1/4 inch. (Not that I am measuring it every day or anything!?!) Scott says it's the perfect buzz cut. And I can already see new eyelashes coming in! Maybe eye-lashes are like teeth and the old ones had to get out of the way for the new ones to come in. (That's my theory and I am sticking to it.) Oh, and quite a few of my friends on breast-cancer.org have reported heavy facial "peach fuzz" prior to new hair growth. I never noticed any and just thought I had lucked out there. Until the other night when Scott congratu-lated me on my fuzzy beard!!! Just what every girl wants to hear! Like I said, it's been a rough week, but armed with my Biblical Red Bull and Mood Enhancer this little fuzzy, buzz-cut Pink Warrior is ready for anything!

Postcard 66
Chicken Fried

Tuesday, September 14, 2010, 2:55 p.m.

So I have been quiet with few postcards over the last few weeks. I have been running this marathon of radiation and have just been "keeping my head down" and pushing through. Yesterday I received some great news. I will be done with my treatments to the whole side tomorrow! I will still have the boosts beginning Thursday but the multi-beam radiation to the whole right breast will be done tomorrow. And honestly, it's not a minute too soon because I believe I have exceeded "extra crispy" status on the Kentucky Fried Chicken scale. The skin under my arm has turned black and is extremely tender. The rest of my right side looks pretty much like a ripe straw-berry. (Can you tell I have my appetite back after chemo? I relate everything to food!) I am really feeling fatigued these days as well. Not sure if it is because I can't get my right side comfortable at night and am not sleeping well, or if the radiation is really taking it out of me.

At any rate, I am happy to see the finish line in front of me. I used my 3 day break over Labor Day weekend to spend a little time down on the farm with my family. Have you ever heard the song "Chicken Fried" by Zac Brown Band? That song comes to mind when I think about my current skin sit-uation and my time on the farm. I may not have grown up in the South, but I grew up in the country. (Just substitute "Indiana" for the "Georgia" part.) The song has a great mes-sage about the "little things" being what really matters and also how grateful we should be for those who sacrificed so much so we can enjoy these small things every day. Both of my amazing brothers were drafted years ago and sacrificed years of their lives to serve our country. I am grateful to them. (But only one of them is bald, like me.)

When brothers agree, no fortress is so strong as their common life.   Antisthenes

Jan and her brothers Gene and Paul

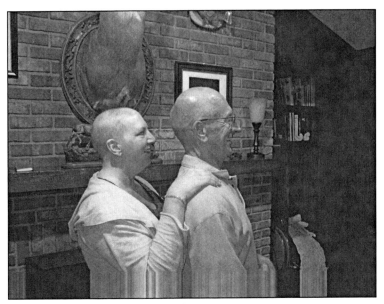

With Gene

Postcard 67

Sheepie – The Sequel: "Unlikely Hero Counteracts Attack Of The Linear Accelerator"

Wednesday, September 15, 2010, 3:57 p.m.

Sheepie is making a comeback! With the pain from the radiation burns under my arm, I have been using my Sheepie again as a source of comfort. (See postcard 16 from March 23, 2010). Who knew she would come in again to save the day? It feels so much better with her just hanging out under my armpit to prevent the rubbing of the tender skin. I "graduated" today from the whole side radiation treatments into the more targeted boost treatments, so I expect the raw, burnt skin to be healing soon as the boosts will be in a different area. It is amazing how this radiation therapy works. I have been doing some reading on the subject and the radiation actually messes with the DNA of the cancer cells, causing them to be unable to group into clusters, preventing the formation of another tumor. The machine I am treated on every day is actually called a "linear accelerator." I lay face up on a board in the center and then the arms of the machine rotate according to the laser beams which line up along my tattoos. I have been having 2 different rays each day. Tomorrow the "boost" treatments will begin a more direct target in one area, the tumor bed that is empty since my lumpectomy. This is to prevent recurrence in the same area which is common. How grateful I am that someone has figured all this out. What a gift of life to me!

*What a wonderful God we have —... the source
of every mercy, and the one who so wonderfully
comforts us and strengthens us in all our trials.
And why does He do this? So that when others
are troubled, ... we can pass on to them the same
help and comfort God has given us.*

2 Corinthians 1:3-4 The Living Bible

Postcard 68
With Bells On

Wednesday, September 22, 2010, 10:08 p.m.

There are lots of bells that I love—the Liberty Bell, jingle bells, the opening bell on the New York Stock Exchange, wedding bells, sleigh bells, the old dinner bell we had on the farm, handbells, Christmas bells, cow bells, "Saved by the Bell," "Silver Bells" and even Taco Bell. But none of them ring as sweet as the bell I rang myself today. Just as the Liberty Bell is a symbol of our American independence, the bell in my radiation treatment office symbolizes freedom. Freedom to move forward in life, focus on other things and put cancer in the rearview mirror. I rang the bell at 7:45 a.m. this morning, signaling the end of my radiation treatments. I find it interesting that I was diagnosed on February 22nd and I finished on September 22nd, exactly 7 months later, just over 200 days. Tonight I am tired so this will be a short post. I am tired from the radiation but because I also had a lovely day celebrating my new "freedom." Tonight I just wanted to share with you the peace that I feel as bells of joy are ringing in my heart tonight.

> *"God's peace is joy resting. His joy is peace dancing."*
> F.F. Bruce

Final Radiation Treatment, September 22

Postcard 69
Taking The Highway To...

Tuesday, September 28, 2010, 9:40 p.m.

Heaven? (well, not on that highway quite yet!); Hair? (unfortunately that destination is still a long way off); a Hysterectomy? (planning that trip later in the year...). For now I am taking the exit marked "Highway to Healing." This road, though it seems downhill, has it's own set of challenges. I can't just "coast" or put it on "cruise control." I need to keep motivated and hopeful and keep moving. The thing is, it would be really easy right now to become somewhat complacent. One week after my final radiation, my skin has peeled off it's last layer (ouch) and now my body is ready to heal, but the state of my mind seems to want to take a detour.

I'm at an unhealthy weight right now and I am cleared to begin a regular exercise program but sleeping in instead of going to the gym sounds nice. And I have achy bones and stiff joints, a lagging effect from the chemo or perhaps the tamoxifen. Yoga or simple stretching exercises would probably really help, but sitting on the couch while I'm watching TV sounds much more pleasant. And many foods and drinks haven't tasted right to me over the last few months, but now they do. Limiting sweets and eliminating alcohol would be the smart choice, but that brownie tastes yummy and a beer with Monday Night Football sounds nice.

Clearly, I need some direction and encouragement. I found some as I read an interesting passage today in my "Streams in the Desert" devotional. It said,

"God's promises and His providence do not lift us from the world of common sense and everyday trials, for it is through these very things that our faith is perfected. And it is in this world that God loves to interweave the golden threads of His love with the twists and turns of our everyday experiences."

Common sense and everyday trials — not very exciting, but what lies on the road ahead now. This road ahead has twists and turns to be sure, but I am confident I will encounter hope, strength, and even joy along this path, the highway to healing.

Postcard 70
One Of The 200,000

Friday, October 1, 2010, 6:46 a.m.

Yesterday on a morning TV news show I listened to the chief medical correspondent talk about a new study regarding mammograms. This new study out of Sweden suggests mammogram screenings should be done each year for every woman after 40; this reverses the findings of a widely communicated study last fall suggesting yearly mammograms be given beginning at age 50.

I remember hearing about the "after 50" study about 10 days AFTER I had my mammogram last fall—the mammogram that detected the lump near my chest wall that I hadn't detected myself. The timing of the mammogram, I truly believe, saved my life. Had I heard the news I didn't need one until after 50 *before* I got my mammogram, I am almost certain I wouldn't have gone. I knew that I had none of the common risk factors. This past week I had the opportunity to thank my general practitioner, Dr. S, at a routine appointment. (Once I got on the cancer track, I never went back for an office visit with her.) She knew of my diagnosis but we hadn't had a chance to talk until yesterday. She ordered the routine mammogram for me last November and I followed through and had it done. The lump was visible on that mammogram. It was cancer. This early detection prevented the cancer from spreading over the next couple years. It allowed us to catch it early, at Stage II. Symptoms of the cancer may not have allowed us to detect it until it was in a much later stage.

I had NO symptoms when I had that mammogram, but having that mammogram made my cancer survivable. I had tears in my eyes when I heard the correspondent yesterday continuing to recommend mammograms beginning at age 50 despite the recent study out of Sweden. Her reasoning was that there is 22 million women to screen between age 40 and 50 and 21.8 million of the women would be fine, only 200,000 would have cancer.

Well, I am one of the 200,000. I am so thankful I had my mammogram. Today, October 1st, begins National Breast Cancer Awareness month. Early detection is key. Don't wait, get screened.

Postcard 71
Vulnerable

Wednesday, October 13, 2010, 11:02 a.m.

I have been enjoying a few days in Boston with my son, Zack. He's a senior in high school and we are here to check out colleges. The time has been really special since it's not often that just the two of us are together. My hair is making an appearance again but it is *very* short. It hasn't even reached "pixie cut" status yet. On our first day here in our hotel room when Zack saw my hair, he was shocked. "MOM! You have hair!" And he was quick to point out I didn't need the wig now.

What? No wig? But I do need it. I get cold. I look so much better with long hair. I paid a lot of money for that wig—I am still getting my money's worth. And for each of my objections, Zack had an answer. "Mom, you look better without the wig. In fact, you look great without the wig. Please don't wear it."

I realized that wearing the wig had become more of a comfort thing... a way for me to "blend in" to my surroundings. Maybe no one will notice me. Maybe no one will see that I had cancer. The truth is that, without the wig, I am vulnerable. Vulnerable to unenlightened comments from strangers and to gawkers (definition of a gawker: "a spectator who stares stupidly without intelligent awareness"). It is a bit cold with only 1/2" hair in Boston, but deep down I am afraid. Scared to be vulnerable. But Zack is right, it's time. I don't *need* the wig. I am going to leave it in my suitcase when I leave our hotel room. With my son walking tall and proud beside me, I will be fine.

"What makes you vulnerable, makes you beautiful."   Brene Brown

In Boston with Zack

Postcard 72
I Left My Heart...And A Few Other Things In Panama City Beach!

Monday, November 1, 2010, 5:26 p.m.

It's been a couple weeks since my last post. I have spent the last lazy days of October in Florida with my husband celebrating his 50th birthday. We had an amazing time. One of Scott's goals before he turned 50 was to purchase a retirement home. He has been on the internet searching nearly every day for about 5 years. This year we decided that our retirement home would be on the gorgeous "emerald" beaches of the Florida panhandle.

After 2 failed offers, we were successful in purchasing a lovely property on the beach. We are planning to begin renting it for weekly rentals and, of course, enjoy it ourselves as much as we can. I am happy to say that my energy level is back up to almost normal so I was able to help get our new place in order. We spent several days unpacking boxes, cleaning, and setting up housekeeping. I fell in love with "our" stretch of Florida beach while I was there and left a piece of my heart there when we left. But I left some other things there that I hadn't planned on. *All* of my *toenails*! Yes—my toenails.

Months ago the oncology nurses warned me that losing nails (finger and toe) was a possibility with chemo, but the treatments were so far behind me I thought that risk was over.

Guess not.

I really couldn't believe it when the first big toenail came loose, but then I quickly realized all 9 of the others weren't far behind. The good news is that my new nails were underneath and already about half way grown. Looking on the bright side, I am pleased that God saw fit to spare me embarrassment by waiting until autumn for them to fall out. I will be wearing mostly closed toe shoes, not my summer flip flops. How TOE-taly awesome!

"To get up when you are down, to fight more intensely when you are struggling; to put in the extra effort when you are in sheer pain, to come back when nobody expects you to, and to stand tall when everyone is pulling you down are what make you a champion." Apoorve Dubey

Postcard 73
"Dude, Where's My Legs?"

Saturday, November 20, 2010, 7:58 a.m.

I am getting back in the swing of things. I am back to work full time, exercising most days and resuming most all of my normal activities. It feels great! This week I am working in Las Vegas for a Scuba Diving Industry Convention called DEMA. It is a 4-day show and I have enjoyed my time here, even though the majority of my time off I have been by myself, exploring, shopping, or working on one of the projects I brought with me.

The only thing about having a lot of time to yourself is that it gives you time to think. Generally, this is great. But maybe "not so much" for a recent cancer survivor who is trying to live each day to its full potential while harboring the thought in the back of her mind that one day the cancer could come back. I have talked to a couple other survivors and found that for most this feeling fades over time, especially with clear regular screenings. I will have my first post-cancer screening on December 2nd, my first mammogram since they discovered the cancer last year.

Maybe it is that pending appointment that has my mind playing tricks on me, sneaking worry and fear into my thoughts. My Friday morning Bible Study is just starting a study called "Living Above Worry and Stress." It's God's perfect timing—I will be learning what He says about worry and fear. Since I have never been a "worry wart" these new troubling and worrisome thoughts about cancer recurrence are foreign to me. I don't think my body knows exactly what to do with them.

In my dreams the other night here at the hotel the cancer was back and I sat straight up in bed and then realized it was a nightmare. I am really beginning to understand what others go through when they are burdened with thoughts of their loved ones overseas in the armed forces, or when their child is diagnosed with a rare disease, or when life takes some other tragic turn. It is our nature to worry about what the future may bring. But it is God's nature to comfort us and He wants us to give all our cares to him so we can focus on each day. The other morning after I had that nightmare I walked down to the lobby of the hotel for a coffee. As I was walking down the "streets of Paris" (my hotel) I saw in man in a wheelchair coming toward me. He was smiling and laughing with the man who was pushing his chair. It was obvious he had no legs. But then I noticed the T-shirt he was wearing, "Dude, Where's My Legs?" How amazing. I passed him just briefly on my way to the coffee shop, but I have been thinking about him ever since. I want to get to the place where he is on *his* journey. I think I am heading the right way as long as I remember these words of God to me:

> *So don't ever worry about tomorrow. After all, tomorrow will worry about itself. Each day has enough trouble of its own.*
> Matthew 6:34 GODS WORD Translation

(I can barely contain my excitement so I can get through this day at the Dive Show. Tomorrow is my "finish line." The day that I have been waiting for all year. Scott and I will be celebrating by attending the American Music Awards in Los Angeles!)

Postcard 74
AMA-zing!!!

Sunday, December 5, 2010, 10:28 a.m.

I have no words to express how much we enjoyed the American Music Awards. Our experience started at the lovely Andaz hotel in West Hollywood. Scott had arranged for a limo transport to the red carpet! With our ticket package purchased on biddingforgood.com we received a window sticker for "Red Carpet Drop Off," two tickets to the show and two tickets to the VIP after party. I spent the better part of the morning getting ready!

The show aired live on the East Coast at 8 p.m. (5 p.m. our time in CA) so we had to start early to get through the red carpet and into our seats by 4 p.m. What to wear?!? Always an issue, right? Scott had a nice black Christian Audiger sports coat and spiffy new blue shirt. Guys are so easy! I spent hours pouring through the racks at Nordstrom Rack and finally settled on a deep teal short dress. But the shoes! That was a problem. I wanted silver shoes but every pair of dressy silver shoes I loved had open toes. (Not the most attractive since I have a toenail issue right now — see postcard 72 from November 1.) Finally, I found the perfect pair of pointy toe silver slingbacks at DSW. A small silver clutch and I was good to go.

Walking up to the show on the red carpet was the first thrill of the evening. All the paparazzi were going crazy and all the shows like *Entertainment Tonight, Inside Edition* and even *Ellen* were represented to interview the stars. As "civilians" we were hurried through the area not allowed to dilly dally too long, but long enough to see some of the stars beautiful gowns! As we entered the Nokia Theatre, beyond the entrance doors the Backstreet Boys were in final rehearsal. The harmonies in the theatre as we sipped a glass of champagne just added to our anticipation.

Finally, when the doors opened, the usher led us down and down and further down front. We couldn't believe it! Our seats were in the 4th row! After most of the guests were seated, the stars started filing in. Jenny McCarthy—GORGEOUS! Julie Benz—a favorite of mine, Justin Bieber—okay he's a teen sensation, but he is a cutie, the BLACK EYED PEAS—LOVE them and their "Ferg-a-licious" Sarah Ferguson (see postcard 34 from April 28), Usher, Taylor Swift, Bon Jovi! They just kept coming! It was hard to believe we were in the same *room,* let alone within 50 feet of all these talented people. When the announcer said, "In 5 seconds we are going live on ABC" everyone started clapping and before I knew it I was looking straight up at Heidi Klum.

The performances were wonderful. My favorites were the Black Eyed Peas and Bon Jovi. Scott liked Santana. By far, the best stage show was Pink. During her song "Raise Your Glass," they were skateboarding on ramps across the stage and throwing girls waaayyyy up in the air, "cheerleader" style. Full of fun and energy. We thought the 3 hour show might seem long, but before we knew it the Backstreet Boys and the New Kids on the Block were closing it out. I didn't want it to be over! But we still had the VIP After Party!

We walked across the street to the after party venue at LA Live, called the "Conga Room" and bumped into Will.I.Am (from the Black Eyed Peas) as we entered. Scott and I aren't as young as we used to be and it's been a while since we have been in a "club" but it didn't take long for our "moves" to come back. A scary thought, I know. The highlight of the night came early for me as Scott noticed Julie Benz (actress on "Dexter," "Ordinary Family" and "Young and the Restless" back in the day) in the room. I got to meet her and talked to her for a sec; she was sweet as I had hoped.

Scott, always the perfect gentleman, managed to grab a barstool for me near the dance floor. Though my legs and feet were aching, I managed to "chair dance" for the next few hours. It seemed the fun would never end. At one point, Scott was mistaken for an actor on "Law and Order." Some lovely young ladies thought they had a real brush with a celebrity (and who were we to ruin their fun!) What a night! The time of our lives.

Pink Warrior Prepped to Party

167

Postcard 75
Just Do It!

Saturday, December 11, 2010, 5:39 p.m.

"Just Do It" has been a phrase used by Nike for many years. You can see it on t-shirts and athletic gear everywhere. My thoughts have been scattered this past week. On the one hand, I am thrilled! I had my first mammogram last week since a year ago when the routine test detected an abnormality. I passed with flying colors! I was given the "all clear—we'll see you again in 6 months." Praise God from whom all blessings flow!

On the other hand, my thoughts have drifted often this past week to Elizabeth Edwards (married to John Edwards, US Senator from North Carolina) who passed away December 7 after a long fight with advanced breast cancer. But for the grace of God, there go I. After listening to an interview with Mrs. Edwards' friends on a morning show this week, I learned that she had let a few years go by without having her annual mammogram testing and by the time her cancer was discovered several years ago it was Stage III.

I, too, had missed a couple years of mammogram screenings in my early 40's, but I was inspired last year by a Facebook status from my nieces. The sisters in North Carolina indicated they had just been to their "save the Ta-Ta's" appointment together. Even though Dr. S, my new physician since our move to San Diego from Aruba, had ordered a mammogram at a recent office visit, I had put it off. Something inside told me when I saw that status not to put it off any longer, but to go in and "get 'er done." So I did.

It was the following week that mainstream media announced a new study that recommended delaying annual mammogram screenings until age 50. By the time I heard that on the news, I already had mine the week before. As long as I live, I will believe that God was in that timing. If I had heard about that study first, I probably wouldn't have gone. And if that was the case, I probably wouldn't have known about the cancer until much later when I felt a lump, when it was already in my nodes, when it was Stage III or more— like Elizabeth Edwards. My prayers go out to her family. She lived a life of great courage and dignity and I hope her young children will understand that when they are older. It is not for us to know why some are saved, spared or why some are taken but only to trust in our loving God and to do our best with what He has entrusted to us. If you, one of your loved ones or someone else you know is "putting off" going to the doctor or having some routine testing, go ahead and *do it now* or encourage your loved one! **JUST DO IT!**

> *So do not fear, for I am with you; do not be dismayed, for I am your God. I will strengthen you and help you; I will uphold you with my righteous right hand.* Isaiah 41:10

Postcard 76
Da Vinci Is My Friend

Sunday, December 12, 2010, 7:39 a.m.

It's not really Leonardo DaVinci, the famous Italian Renaissance genius (painter, sculptor, scientist, mathematician, inventor), but rather his namesake—the Da Vinci hysterectomy. Tomorrow I will be checking into Scripps Memorial in La Jolla to undergo this procedure. As my surgeon put it, "this is not your Momma's hysterectomy." My surgeon will be using a robotic device and 4 small incisions for this laparoscopic surgery. The robotic surgical system used is called Da Vinci because the original robot prototype in 1997 was nicknamed "Lenny" after Leonardo Da Vinci.

Now a more advanced and fully tested robot system is used for a variety of "Da Vinci" procedures. I opted for the surgery knowing that the estrogen my ovaries produce may fuel any cancer cells that have lingered following chemo. Furthermore, after learning that my diagnosis of ER+ breast cancer puts me at an increased risk for ovarian or uterine cancer, it just seemed like the right decision to make. I have surgery in the morning and will be spending the night, but expect to be released early Tuesday. As I contemplated the surgery, I must admit feeling a bit apprehensive; however, as I researched the procedure online I became comfortable with the surgery and even thankful that my hospital offers this less invasive, more accurate option.

In the words of Da Vinci himself: "The acquisition of knowledge is always of use to the intellect, because it may thus drive out useless things and retain the good. For nothing can be loved or hated unless it is first known." My sentiments exactly!

Postcard 77
Hormones Gone Haywire?

Friday, December 24, 2010, 6:38 p.m.

A welcome Christmas package arrived today from my "Hyster-Sisters." Who knew there was a whole website and support group devoted to care for women facing hysterectomies? (HysterSisters.com, strange name, nice website) After my surgery last week, I have been experiencing some discomfort in my belly. I have 5 small incisions on my tummy which don't give me sharp pains, but if I am on my feet too much, then I get this sensation that my stitches are ripping or bursting. Not a lot of fun.

I ran into an acquaintance last week and we started chatting. She had a hysterectomy a few years ago and had the same sensations. She told me about the website so I checked it out and I ended up ordering a belly band. I put it on straight out of the box and felt immediate support and pain relief. In the box with the belly band was a small booklet. I remember reading a similar book years ago called, "What to expect when you are expecting" but this was titled, "What to expect when you have a hysterectomy." Looked like good information so I started to skim the pages. A paragraph caught my eye, "Hormones gone haywire!" That's me! I had just been telling Scott earlier today how I am so close to tears at any moment and at the same time so close to fury. It is as if my passion at any given moment has been raised exponentially.

The paragraph in the pamphlet described in detail how the surgery alone can render any woman's emotions defenseless and exposed. Since I am also continuing to take tamoxifen, which is blocking any estrogen production I have left, the symptoms seem exacerbated. It's a wonder I am not a basket case. And of course I would be "Miss Emotional" at Christmastime, probably the most moving, tender and heart-warming time of the year. Over the past couple days, my thoughts have wandered to any number of Christmases that I have shared, shared with my children when they were little, shared with my family when I was growing up, and shared with my husband no matter where we were living. And my thoughts also went back to that first Christmas when Mary brought forth her first born son, Jesus. I am sure her hormones had "gone haywire" as well since they do so during pregnancy. I am sure she was full of emotion. Yet Luke 2 where the Christmas story is detailed tells us, "but Mary treasured up all these things and pondered them in her heart." (v. 19)

I know that I, like Mary, have all these emotions for a reason, but I also know that I can exercise self-control and keep the expression of my feelings in check. I can follow Mary's example and treasure up all these things and ponder them in my heart. Certainly I will shed a tear or two as I always do at Christmas—when I remember fondly the Christmas Eves of my youth and the traditions my mother perpetuated, when I think about my kids when they were little, their innocence as they peered wide-eyed at their bulging stockings and checked to see if Santa had eaten the cookies they left for him, when I experience the tenderness of my husband as he kisses me under the mistletoe; but I will hold at bay the anger that strikes me when a fellow shopper snags my parking spot or cuts in line at the checkout, the worry I feel when my kids board the plane and have to travel through the snow storm, the frustration I feel when I run out of wrapping paper at midnight on Christmas Eve and still have 2 gifts to wrap. I will do less blurting and bellowing and more reflecting and meditating. More *pondering*. I will keep the "Mary" in Christmas! So with much joy, nearly bursting from my heart, I wish you all a *very* Merry Christmas!

> *Let love and faithfulness never leave you; bind them around your neck, write them on the tablet of your heart.*   Proverbs 3:3

Postcard 78
Surprised by Joy

Monday, January 24, 2011, 5:44 p.m.

A couple days ago my baby boy turned 18. He has grown into a fine young man. He is loving, kind, smart, happy. All the things you hope for your child as they are growing up. The "mom" in me had to be there for this milestone (he is in Ohio with his dad, finishing up his senior year of high school and I am in California) so I flew out to surprise him!

My daughter, Savannah and I "camped" outside his workplace Friday night waiting for him to finish his shift. We watched him mopping the floors at Arby's, working hard, unaware that we were in the parking lot. When he finally got off and walked out to the parking lot, I stepped out into his line of sight and said, "Hey, Zack." He looked and then did a double take and then screamed, "MOM!!!" What a moment! My heart was literally bursting with joy.

I have noticed recently that I have felt more deeply the emotions associated with events that are happening in my daily life. I have posted about the tears and have blamed it all on hormones. But I have to admit that the joys in my life have increased exponentially as well. This "heart-bursting" feeling, full of joy, has become common over the last few months, even in the *simple* joys of life. Over the Christmas holiday hearing my kids laughing together in another room, sitting quietly holding hands with my husband on the couch, shopping for treasures at the consignment store with my sister-in-law, sharing a mojito and a NFL playoff game with a girlfriend, coffee and a bagel with my sister—all of these common occurrences, but I have experienced great joy in these moments and many others.

I read something this week in my favorite devotional, "Streams in the Desert" that may explain. The passage also gives me great comfort and hope. The devotion suggests that the sorrows that we experience in life cause our heart to expand so that the joy we experience is greater as well. The many sorrows in my life, such as the loss of my father at age 11 and my mother at 16, as well as a painful divorce and most recently my breast cancer diagnosis, have all worked within me to expand my heart and to make room for more and deeper joy. The devotional says,

> "Sorrow is God's tool to plow the depths of the soul, that it may yield richer harvests....In the same way we say, 'Blessed is the night, for it reveals the stars to us,' we can say, 'Blessed is sorrow, for it reveals God's comfort.'" I love this analogy from the devotional: "A flood once washed away a poor man's home, taking with it everything he owned in the world. He stood at the scene of his great loss, brokenhearted and discouraged. Yet, after the waters had subsided, he saw something shining in the riverbanks that the flood had washed bare. 'It looks like gold,' he said. And it was gold. The storm that had impoverished him made him rich. So it is oftentimes in life."

Whatever sorrow life brings may joy follow, in abundance.

Sorrow is better than laughter, for by a sad countenance the heart is made better.
Ecclesiastes 7:3 NKJV

Postcard 79
The Year Of The What?

Thursday, February 3, 2011, 3:50 p.m.

Today is the Chinese New Year and thus begins the "Year of the Rabbit." Ancient teachings suggest that the Year of the Rabbit is one of peace or at least a respite from conflict and war. I have been wondering, what will 2011 bring for me?

It is already February and I feel a bit restless wondering what the year will bring or even more intriguing — what should I pursue in 2011? From the looks of the growth of my new "fluff-a-licious" hair, I could accurately predict "2011— The Year of the Poodle." Certainly last year was my "Year of the Pink Warrior." I didn't plan it that way, of course, but that's the way I will always remember 2010. Just as I will always remember 1982 as the "Year My Mother Passed Away," 1993 as the "Year of Zack," 1996 as the "Year of Savannah," and 2004 as the "Year of my Miracle" (the year I met Scott).

Other years blur together, but the ones that brought major life changes are remembered. Surviving breast cancer makes me realize that life is such a gift, a gift that we often forget and take for granted even. And in my heart I am committed to making each year in my future count — count for something meaningful and enduring. I no longer want the years to fly by in a blur. I want each year to be special, important, remembered. In 2011, my son will graduate high school and go away to college, also two of my nieces will be married. I know these milestones will always be remembered and will make 2011 a special year of celebration, with heartwarming family moments shared among those I love. Of course I am looking forward to all that, but today I am also looking inside myself trying to discover how I can make changes in my own life and a make difference in the lives of others during 2011.

Will 2011 be the "Year of Skinny Jan," the "Year of Jan Walks the Susan G. Komen 3Day," the "Year of Author Jan" or the "Year of Volunteer Jan" ? Throughout the coming weeks, I will be praying for guidance, direction and determination to make this a Year. A Year to be remembered.

"What lies behind us and what lies before us are tiny matters compared to what lies within us."
Ralph Waldo Emerson

Postcard 80
I Need New Shoes!

Tuesday, February 22, 2011, 10:39 a.m.

I admit it. I *love* shoes! Most women do, I think. My husband is perplexed by the fascination, but he humors me and often chooses a special pair of shoes for me for a birthday or Christmas gift. We live within walking distance from a Marshall's Mega Shoe Store and this has become my primary source for new shoes. They have an amazing shoe clearance section where I found the most wonderful Kate Spade pumps for $29! Who can resist that?

The variety of shoes I own has required my organized husband to purchase a shoe rack and 2 "over the closet door" shoe hangers. Recently Scott and I had a discussion that I probably had enough shoes for a while and should just enjoy what I have. I agreed. So I have been avoiding the shoe displays at Marshalls. As he reads this, he will be relieved to know that I am not talking about needing new UGGS or Kate Spades. Our pastor recently did a sermon series on the "Armor of God." I had heard of this concept before. When I was very small, I remember "marching" around in Sunday School to the hymn "Onward Christian Soldiers" and in Vacation Bible School we sang a catchy tune called, "I'm in the Lord's Army." I remember in my parochial school education hearing about the "belt of truth" and the "sword of the spirit" (from Ephesians 6), but somehow I didn't remember anything from way back about shoes.

In his sermon on Super Bowl Sunday, our Pastor started talking about the football players that would be taking to the field that day—how their feet were "fitted" with custom cleats so they could hold their ground and not be "bowled over" by the opposing team. He also shared that in Bible times the "warriors" of the day would put nails through the sole of their sandals so they could hold their ground. Then Pastor Jim talked about the things in life that try to "bowl us over." We have all been there. There has been something coming at us so hard we are afraid we can't stand up against it.

Maybe it is problems in a relationship, maybe it is health of a child or ourselves, maybe an unexpected death in the family, maybe a merciless boss at work — for me, a cancer diagnosis exactly one year ago today. We are all in need of "custom cleats" to stand firm in times of trouble. Ephesians 6:15 says, "For shoes, put on the peace that comes from the Good News, so that you will be fully prepared." That's really the only pair of shoes I need, "the cleats of peace." And where do we get them? Well, not at Marshalls.

In Philippians 4: 6-7 it says peace comes from going to God in every situation:

> *"Do not be anxious about anything, but in every situation, by prayer and petition, with thanks-giving, present your requests to God. And the peace of God, which transcends all under-standing, will guard your hearts and your minds in Christ Jesus."*

The peace of God which "transcends all understanding" is what holds us up when we are in danger of being "bowled over." I'm not much of an athlete but I am going to try to put on these "cleats" daily.

> *You will keep in perfect peace those whose minds are steadfast, because they trust in You.*
>
> Isaiah 26:3

Postcard 81
First Hair Cut

Thursday, March 10, 2011, 2:24 p.m.

I remember both of my children's first hair cuts. It was exciting for *me* (for **them**—not so much). I was careful to save a lock of their golden curls for their baby book. The first hair cut, like their first word, was a milestone, a right of passage, as they were growing up.

Today I will have my first hair cut of my new "chemo" locks. They are far from golden, but there are plenty of curls. Just like my daughter's hair when she was little. I remember telling the hair stylist not to cut off her precious curls. It took her long enough to get them! In her 1-year-old photos she is pretty much bald. I feel the same way today. I trust my friend Mary to give me a great cut. But there is part of me that wants to say, "Don't cut too much! It took a long time to get this much hair—enough for a cut." When my kids got their first hair cut, I would hold them on my lap since they were so scared of the scissors. The "Mom" in me relished the time spent holding each of them during this milestone. I would comfort them and say, "It's going to be okay. I am right here with you. You are growing up, so now you need a hair cut!" When they were all done, I was SO proud of them and usually got them a lollipop or another little treat for being good.

I know that today my own heavenly Father will "hold me on His lap" and say, "it's okay. I am here with you. You are moving passed your cancer diagnosis, back into life, so now

you need a hair cut." And I know I will feel His love and comfort too.

*Consider this: The Father has given us his love.
He loves us so much that we are actually called
God's dear children. And that's what we are.*
1 John 3:1 GOD'S WORD Translation

Postcard 82
Tsunami Survival

Saturday, April 9, 2011, 6:41 p.m.

A few weeks ago tsunami warnings were issued for San Diego County following the earthquake and subsequent tsunami in Sendai, Japan. I live about 1 ½ miles from the west coast of the US. I live on the 12th floor. Far enough away and high enough to be safe, right? As the warning came in, I contemplated whether to go to my Friday morning Bible Study at our church. The church is just a few blocks from the beach. I decided to stay home. Though all my sensibilities told me that a giant wave would not come ashore in my neighborhood, I kept thinking in the back of my mind, "I am sure that is what all those precious people in Japan thought. And then it did." In the days since the disaster in Japan, we have seen images we never thought we would see—images of complete and utter chaos and devastation. The totality of the destruction boggles the mind. I have seen the images on TV of families torn apart and searching for loved ones and I have tried to put myself in their shoes. What would I do? How would I feel? How would I cope? What do you do when life as you know it ends and a new reality emerges, full of challenges and never-imagined circumstances? And the thought came to me. I have experienced my own personal "tsunami." My tsunami was called "cancer."

The same feelings of helplessness, fear of the unknown and adjustment to a new reality are very much a part of a cancer diagnosis. And it happens every day to countless numbers of people, people just like me, who get that phone call and hear the "c" word. Since the tsunami in Japan, conversations have started about the safety of nuclear power all over the world. Fundraisers are in full swing to help the victims and the world begins to a look and tries to make changes. Changes that will result in a better outcome should a devastating tsunami ever happen again.

In the same way, on a personal level, I have been considering how I can make some changes. Changes that can impact my own life so that I never have to face the "cancer" tsunami again—like eating more fish, less beef; exercising more; keeping up with my oncologist checkups; switching to organic milk and produce and non-GMO products. As I am trying to make my own changes, I received the news that the wife of a friend was just diagnosed with breast cancer—her "tsunami" is just beginning.

More than ever, I realize I want to help others who may face a breast cancer "tsunami" in the future. Recently, I read a brief article on the Susan G. Komen foundation. This article featured 8 recent developments in the fight against breast cancer. It pointed out that portion of the funding for these new scientific developments in the fight against breast cancer came from Susan G. Komen. As I read, I was stunned to realize that I had personally benefitted from 6 of the 8 new developments listed. Those who have worked so hard to raise funds for this cause have made an impact. They have made an impact in my own life.

And in that moment that I decided. I would register for the Susan G. Komen 3-Day 60 Mile Walk. People just like me took bold steps years ago and raised funds for research so that I could benefit. I know some of these people have lost their battle and have not survived their "tsunami." I am surviving and I want others to survive as well. What if the money raised now help to develop treatments or even a cure that could impact my daughter, nieces or granddaughters?

Did you know that "each year more than 400,000 people worldwide die from breast cancer?"[1] Did you know that "breast cancer is the most frequently diagnosed cancer and the leading cause of cancer death among women world-wide?"[2] Do you realize that "one in 8 women in the United States will be diagnosed with breast cancer in her lifetime?"[3] These statistics are shocking.

Before I myself heard the words, "You have breast cancer" I had no idea. I have journeyed into world I never dreamed I would experience and have lived to tell about it, to share. So many have walked the same road. I hope and pray that it will many years before I see my Lord and find out why I survived this journey and others have not. But until then I will hold the memories of my journey close at heart, to comfort those along the same path. Together we can work to eliminate breast cancer for our loved ones and future children by supporting those who are developing new treatments daily and those in search of a cure. And we can help one another by reaching out, by being real, by becoming vulnerable and sharing of ourselves in support of each other. It is the best way to travel—together.

6-0 MILES COMPLETE! Komen 3-Day 2011, San Diego, CA

Jan and Savannah, Race for the Cure Los Angeles 2012

Scott and Jan, 60 Miles Together, Komen 3-Day 2013, San Diego, CA

Triumph! Walking past Jan's Cancer Center during the Susan G. Komen
3-Day 2013, San Diego, CA

ENDNOTES

1: American Cancer Society Global Cancer Facts and Figures, 2nd Edition.
2: Institute for Health Metrics and Evaluation, University of Washington, The Challenge Ahead: Progress and Setbacks in Breast and Cervical Cancer, September 2011. Also see: Breast and Cervical Cancer in 187 Countries between 1980 and 2010: a systemic analysis. www.thelancet.com September 15, 2011.
3: Breast Cancer Facts and Figures 2011-2012 ACS.

You'll Never Walk Alone

R. Rogers/O. Hammerstein II

When you walk through a storm
Hold your head up high
And don't be afraid of the dark
At the end of the storm
Is a golden sky
And the sweet silver song of the lark
Walk on through the wind
Walk on through the rain
Though your dreams be tossed and blown
Walk on walk on with hope in your heart
And you'll never walk alone
You'll never walk alone

The Journey Continues.

*J*an and her husband, Scott, are currently living on Maui in the Hawaiian Islands. Scott has been transferred by his employer 3 times since Jan's diagnosis in 2010, yet Jan continues to see her health care professionals at Scripps Green Cancer Center in La Jolla, California for her bi-annual checkups. In 2015, she is celebrating 2 incredible milestones — reaching age 50 and 5 years cancer-free. Jan is a "three-peat" walker in the Susan G. Komen 3-Day 60 Mile Walk. She has walked every step, 60 miles each year, to benefit breast cancer research in 2011, 2013 (along with her husband Scott), and in 2015 (with her daughter Savannah). Her family has participated in Race for the Cure in Los Angeles and San Diego as well as volunteering for the Komen Affiliate in Los Angeles County for several years. Together, the Allens have raised more than $15,000 for breast cancer research. In addition, a portion of the proceeds of the sale of "Have Breast Cancer, Will Travel" will be donated. Jan is available for speaking engagements and presentations on women's health issues as well as mothering, step-parenting and, of course, travel. Join Jan as her journey continues at <u>jansjour-neyblog.wordpress.com</u> and visit her website at <u>havebreast-cancerwilltravel.com</u>. Her deepest desire is that no woman walk alone.

> "As I have loved you, so you must love one
> another."   John 13:34b

Appendix A:
Breast Cancer Survival Rates and Staging

1) Survival rates are often used by doctors as a standard way of discussing a person's prognosis (outlook). Some patients with breast cancer may want to know the survival statistics for people in similar situations, while others may not find the numbers helpful, or may even not want to know them.

The 5-year observed survival rate refers to the percentage of patients who live at least 5 years after being diagnosed with cancer. Many of these patients live much longer than 5 years after diagnosis.

A relative survival rate (like the numbers below) compares the observed survival with what would be expected for people without the cancer. This helps to correct for the deaths caused by something besides cancer and is a more accurate way to describe the effect of cancer on survival.

(Relative survival rates are at least as high as observed survival, and in most cases are higher.)

In order to get 5-year survival rates, doctors have to look at people who were treated at least 5 years ago. Improvements in treatment since then may result in a more favorable outlook for people now being diagnosed with breast cancer.

Survival rates are often based on previous outcomes of large numbers of people who had the disease, but they cannot predict what will happen in any particular person's case. Many other factors may affect a person's outlook, such as your age and health, the presence of hormone receptors on the cancer cells, the treatment received, and how well the cancer responds to treatment. Your doctor can tell you how the numbers below may apply to you, as he or she is familiar with the aspects of your particular situation.

The available statistics do not divide survival rates by all of the substages, such as IA and IB. The rates for these substages are likely to be close to the rate for the overall stage. For example, the survival rate for stage IA is likely to be slightly higher than that listed for stage I, while the survival rate for stage IB would be expected to be slightly lower.

It is also important to realize that these statistics are based on the stage of the cancer when it was first diagnosed. These do not apply to cancers that later come back or spread, for example.

The rates below come from the National Cancer Institute's SEER database. They are based on the previous version of AJCC staging. In that version stage II also included patients that would now be considered stage IB.

Stage	Five Year Survival Rate
0	100%
I	100%
II	93%
III	72%
IV	22%

Stage is expressed in Roman numerals from stage I (the least advanced stage) to stage IV (the most advanced stage). *See 2) below.

SOURCE: American Cancer Society, last revised 6/10/2015

2) Breast Cancer Staging is based on four characteristics: the size of the cancer, whether the cancer is invasive or non-invasive, whether the cancer is in the lymph nodes, and whether the cancer has spread to other parts of the body beyond the breast. You may also see or hear certain words to describe the stage of the breast cancer: Local–The cancer is confined within the breast. Regional–The lymph nodes, primarily those in the armpit, are involved. Distant–The cancer is found in other parts of the body as well.

Stage 0–In stage 0, there is no evidence of cancer cells or non-cancerous abnormal cells breaking out of the part of the breast in which they started, or getting through to or invading neighboring normal tissue.

Stage I–Stage I is describes invasive breast cancer (cancer cells are breaking through or invading normal surrounding breast tissue) and Stage I is divided into subcategories known as IA and IB. Stage IA describes invasive breast cancer in which: the tumor measures up to 2 centimeters AND the cancer has not spread outside the breast; no lymph nodes are involved. Stage IB describes invasive breast cancer in which: there is no tumor in the breast; instead small groups of cancer cells — larger than 0.2 millimeter but not larger than 2 millimeters — are found in the lymph nodes OR there is a tumor in the breast that is no larger than 2 centimeters, and there are small groups of cancer cells — larger than 0.2 millimeter but not larger than 2 millimeters — in the lymph nodes.

Stage II–Stage II is divided into subcategories known as IIA and IIB. Stage IIA describes invasive breast cancer in which: no tumor can be found in the breast, but cancer (larger than 2 millimeters) is found in 1 to 3 axillary lymph nodes (the lymph nodes under the arm) or in the lymph nodes near the breast bone (found in a sentinel node biopsy) OR the tumor measures 2 centimeters or smaller and has spread to the axillary lymph nodes OR the tumor is larger than 2 centimeters but not larger than 5 centimeters and has not spread to the axillary lymph nodes. Stage IIB describes invasive breast cancer in which the tumor is larger than 2 centimeters but not larger than 5 centimeters; small groups of breast cancer cells — larger than 0.2 millimeter but not larger than 2 millimeters — are found in the lymph nodes OR the tumor is larger than 2 centimeters but not larger than 5 centimeters; cancer has spread to 1 to 3 axillary lymph nodes or to lymph nodes near the breast bone (found during sentinel node biopsy) OR the tumor is larger than 5 centimeters but has not spread to the axillary lymph nodes.

Stage III–Stage III is divided into subcategories known as IIIA, IIIB, and IIIC. Stage IIIA describes invasive breast cancer in which either: no tumor is found in the breast or the tumor may be any size; cancer is found in 4 to 9 axillary lymph nodes or in the lymph nodes near the breastbone (found during imaging tests or a physical exam) OR the tumor is larger than 5 centimeters; small groups of breast cancer cells (larger than 0.2 millimeter but not larger than 2 millimeters) are found in the lymph nodes OR the tumor is larger than 5 centimeters; cancer has spread to 1 to 3 axillary lymph nodes or to the lymph nodes near the breastbone (found during a sentinel lymph node biopsy). Stage IIIB describes invasive breast cancer in which: the tumor may be any size and has spread to the chest wall and/or skin of the breast and caused swelling or an ulcer AND may have spread to up to 9 axillary lymph nodes OR may have spread to lymph nodes near the breastbone. Inflammatory breast cancer is considered Stage IIIB. Stage IIIC describes invasive breast cancer in which: there may be no sign of cancer in the breast or, if there is a tumor, it may be any size and may have spread to the chest wall and/or the skin of the breast AND the cancer has spread to 10 or more axillary lymph nodes OR the cancer has spread to lymph nodes above or below the collarbone OR the cancer has spread to axillary lymph nodes or to lymph nodes near the breastbone.

Stage IV–Stage IV describes invasive breast cancer that has spread beyond the breast and nearby lymph nodes to other organs of the body, such as the lungs, distant lymph nodes, skin, bones, liver, or brain. You may hear the words "advanced" and "metastatic" used to describe stage IV breast cancer. Cancer may be stage IV at first diagnosis or it can be a recurrence of a previous breast cancer that has spread to other parts of the body.

Source: breastcancer.org last revised March 3, 2015

Appendix B:
BRCA Gene Testing

What are *BRCA1* and *BRCA2*?

BRCA1 and *BRCA2* are human genes that produce tumor suppressor proteins. These proteins help repair damaged <u>DNA</u> and, therefore, play a role in ensuring the stability of the <u>cell</u>'s genetic material. When either of these genes is mutated, or altered, such that its protein product either is not made or does not function correctly, DNA damage may not be repaired properly. As a result, cells are more likely to develop additional genetic alterations that can lead to cancer.

Specific inherited mutations in *BRCA1* and *BRCA2* increase the risk of female breast and ovarian cancers, and they have been associated with increased risks of several additional types of cancer. Together, *BRCA1* and *BRCA2* mutations account for about 20 to 25 percent of *hereditary* breast cancers (Easton DF. *Breast Cancer Research* 1999) and about

5 to 10 percent of *all* breast cancers (Campeau p.m., Foulkes WD, Tischkowitz MD. *Human Genetics* 2008). In addition, mutations in *BRCA1* and *BRCA2* account for around 15 percent of ovarian cancers overall (Pal T, Permuth-Wey J, Betts JA. *Cancer* 2005). Breast and ovarian cancers associated with *BRCA1* and *BRCA2* mutations tend to develop at younger ages than their nonhereditary counterparts.

A harmful *BRCA1* or *BRCA2* mutation can be inherited from a person's mother or father. Each child of a parent who carries a mutation in one of these genes has a 50 percent chance (or 1 chance in 2) of inheriting the mutation. The effects of mutations in *BRCA1* and *BRCA2* are seen even when a person's second copy of the gene is normal.

Source: National Cancer Institute

CPSIA information can be obtained
at www.ICGtesting.com
Printed in the USA
FSOW01n2218211015
12445FS